The International Supply of Medicines

A conference sponsored by the
American Enterprise Institute for Public Policy Research

The International Supply of Medicines

Implications of U.S. Regulatory Reform

Edited by Robert B. Helms

American Enterprise Institute for Public Policy Research
Washington, D.C.

Library of Congress Cataloging in Publication Data
Main entry under title:

The International supply of medicines.

    (AEI symposia ; 80-E)
    Includes bibliographical references.
    1. Drug trade—Congresses. 2. Pharmaceutical
policy—United States—Congresses. 3. Trade secrets—
Congresses. 4. Underdeveloped areas—Drug trade—
Congresses. I. Helms, Robert B. II. American
Enterprise Institute for Public Policy Research.
III. Series: American Enterprise Institute for
Public Policy Research. AEI symposia ; 80-E.
HD9665.5.I65   382′.456151′0973   80-23464
ISBN 0-8447-2190-5
ISBN 0-8447-2191-3 (pbk.)

AEI symposia 80-E

Printed in the United States of America

Contents

PART THREE
MEDICINES FOR THE THIRD WORLD

Contributors

Daniel K. Benjamin
Associate Professor of Economics
University of Washington, Seattle

Francis J. Blee
Corporate Economist
SmithKline Corporation

Josef C. Brada
Associate Professor of Economics
Arizona State University

Kenneth W. Clarkson
Law and Economics Center
University of Miami

Fay H. Dworkin
Economic Analysis Staff
Food and Drug Administration

Henry G. Grabowski
Professor of Economics
Duke University

Klaus von Grebmer
Economist
CIBA-GEIGY
Basel, Switzerland

Robert B. Helms
Director, Center for Health Policy Research
American Enterprise Institute

John Jennings
Director of International Affairs
Food and Drug Administration

Edmund W. Kitch
Professor of Law
University of Chicago

Carole Kitti
Policy Analyst
National Science Foundation

David L. Ladd
Law and Economics Center
University of Miami

William MacLeod
Law and Economics Center
University of Miami

Stephen P. Magee
Professor of Finance
University of Texas, Austin

Edwin Mansfield
Professor of Economics
University of Pennsylvania

Rachel McCulloch
Associate Professor of Economics
University of Wisconsin

John E. S. Parker
Senior Lecturer in Economics
Otago University, Dunedin, New Zealand

Rolf R. Piekarz
Directorate for Scientific, Technological, and International Affairs
National Science Foundation

William Treharne
Vice President, Public Affairs
Pfizer International, Inc.

*This conference was held at
the American Enterprise Institute for Public Policy Research
in Washington, D.C. on September 15, 1978*

Foreword

This volume presents the proceedings of the first of two conferences sponsored by AEI's Center for Health Policy Research to address the major economic issues relating to the reform of this country's system of drug regulation. The issues addressed deal primarily with the international aspects of the debate, while a later volume, *Drugs and Health: Economic Issues and Policy Objectives*, will concentrate on domestic issues.

The contributors to this volume, in analyzing the effects of our domestic regulation on the world trade of pharmaceuticals, also present a detailed view of some major factors affecting world trade of all commodities. Among other topics, they discuss the role of international patent agreements in promoting research and development, the factors that affect where and how multinational firms carry out research and production, the importance of product information on a company's ability to compete internationally, and the potential, as well as the problems, presented by new markets in developing countries. These topics are of concern to all those interested in world trade and development, especially in the trade of the highly technical products that make up such a large proportion of U.S. exports.

The contributors have also succeeded in bringing the debate about drug regulation out of its domestic shell. Debates in this country have scarcely addressed the effects of domestic regulation on the ability of our industries to compete in international markets. With our growing concern about the decline in real growth, the slowdown in productivity, and the rate of inflation, there is a realization that our goals for domestic safety and environmental improvement must be pursued in a more careful and rational way. As a wealthy country, we may indeed be able to afford a cleaner environment and safer products than other countries, but international markets are too competitive for us to be reckless in this pursuit. The real challenge to public policy is one that is similar to the challenge faced by any entrepreneur—how to carry out the objective in the most efficient (or least costly) way.

FOREWORD

To achieve regulatory reform that will bring our desire to avoid excessive environmental and health risks into balance with our desire to maintain a healthy economy, we must understand how our own industries compete in international markets and how regulatory agencies affect this competition. We think this volume makes a worthwhile contribution to that understanding.

WILLIAM J. BAROODY, JR.
President
American Enterprise Institute
  for Public Policy Research
August 1980

Preface

Objectives

The international trade of commodities has fascinated scholars for centuries. In fact, the fundamental theories of economics were formulated by early economists who were attempting to explain whether government restrictions on international trade would leave a country poorer, as Adam Smith contended, or richer, as the mercantilists contended. The curiosity of these early economists gave us knowledge that is still applicable to contemporary policy debates, even those regarding the reform of U.S. regulatory policy toward drugs. David Ricardo's example of the trade in cloth and wine between Portugal and England in the early nineteenth century presents the same not-so-obvious message as do the contemporary textbook examples of Linus and Charlie Brown trading candy and cokes—individuals everywhere can have more goods to consume if each country specializes more in what it can produce cheaply and trades some of these products for those of other countries.

International trade takes place because the resources and talents required to produce goods are not distributed around the world in the same way as peoples' desires to consume them. Each commodity has its own unique pattern of trade, and drugs offer a most interesting illustration. There is a demand for drugs wherever people suffer from illnesses treatable by medicines. But the supply is concentrated in the industrial countries that have the essential technology for discovery and production.

The mercantilist policies that prevailed in England, France, and other countries in the eighteenth century assumed that a country could gain wealth only by accumulating gold and silver (specie). By promoting exports and restricting imports, the government could contribute to this accumulation. A premium was placed on self-sufficiency, that is, on not being too dependent on other countries for the import of various commodities, an idea that is still very much with us today in the debate about drugs in international trade.

Adam Smith's idea—that international trade could be mutually beneficial to the trading countries and promote their economic growth —directly challenged mercantilism. He and the classical economists who followed him showed the folly of thinking that all nations could gain from mercantilist policies. Public policies that restrict trade, it was shown, retard the process of specialization that reduces the cost of production. This volume attempts to deal with a variant of this policy question: How can government policies promote the efficient production of medicines, especially in the industrial countries, where most research, development, and production now take place? While the old mercantilist concerns about relying too much on imports are still alive, the debate now concentrates on government policies affecting the export of drugs. Several authors in this volume express concern that regulatory policies inhibit domestic firms' ability to supply these exports. Is the United States losing its comparative advantage in the production of drugs? This is a difficult question to answer, especially when U.S. government policy explicitly attempts to improve the safety of U.S. produced drugs. There is little doubt that the Food and Drug Administration's requirements increase the costs of both research and production. What is in doubt is whether the benefits of improved safety are worth the cost of the reduced flow of new drugs, and whether the rest of the world demands the degree of safety we strive for.

This volume takes up several aspects of this debate, especially the effects of proposed changes in U.S. domestic policy on the international trade of drugs. In particular, it looks at evidence about changes in trade patterns among the major producing countries, the effects of changing laws on patents and on the release of proprietary information, and the international response of U.S. firms to changing regulatory policies. The special problems of supplying drugs to less developed countries are also considered.

Adam Smith has provided us not only with a fundamental insight about how international trade promotes economic growth, but also with an additional lesson relevant to the debate about the reform of U.S. regulatory policy. In Smith's criticism of mercantilism, and in particular his criticism of laws that restricted imports of corn, he pointed out a fundamental difference between the way uninhibited markets work and the way governments seek to operate markets. In explaining the behavior of an individual in a private market, Smith, in his most famous passage, said:

He generally, indeed, neither intends to promote the public interest, nor knows how much he is promoting it . . . he is in this, as in many other cases, led by an invisible hand to promote an end which was no part of his intention. . . .[1]

Even though Smith could describe businessmen as "an order of men . . . who have generally an interest to deceive and even to oppress the public,"[2] he viewed them as being constrained by the discipline of the marketplace. But he reserved his strongest criticism for "that insidious and crafty animal, vulgarly called the statesman or politician."[3]

> The statesman, who should attempt to direct private people in what manner they ought to employ their capitals, would not only load himself with a most unnecessary attention, but assume an authority which could safely be trusted, not only to no single person, but to no council or senate whatever, and which would nowhere be so dangerous as in the hands of a man who had folly and presumption enough to fancy himself fit to exercise it.[4]

Although businessmen, politicians, and regulatory officials have probably refined their behavior since the rough-and-tumble days of the late eighteenth century, these quotations still bear on the current debate about regulatory reform in general and about drug regulation in particular. Smith was saying not that we should put blind faith in businessmen but that we should put more faith in the rewards and punishments of the *marketplace*, which would induce the business sector to satisfy consumer demands in the most efficient way.

Even though most people would be willing to rely upon the marketplace for corn, top hats, and buggy whips, they might question the wisdom of its use for products of modern corporations that can bestow both benefits and adverse effects on users. Not only must the marketplace provide the optimum amount of each product and the optimum variety of products, it must also provide the optimum amount of information about the product to satisfy consumer demands about the safety and effectiveness of the product. The basic policy question then becomes whether the marketplace or a government agency should provide this optimum amount of safety. Will modern drug firms under-

---

[1] Adam Smith, *The Wealth of Nations*, 1776 (Modern Library Edition, 1937), p. 423. This section on Adam Smith and mercantilism relies on the interpretation and quotes by Thomas Sowell in *Economics: Analysis and Issues* (Glenview, Illinois: Scott, Foresman and Co., 1971), pp. 323–327.

[2] Adam Smith, *The Wealth of Nations*, p. 250.

[3] Ibid., p. 435.

[4] Ibid., p. 423.

emphasize safety and impose undue risks on consumers? Or, will the FDA overemphasize safety and consequently reduce the resources available to find new cures?

These are complex questions. In the editor's opinion, Adam Smith's assessment of the market and of the ability of government agencies to improve its performance is essentially correct. Studies of regulatory agencies show that their reward structure discourages their employees from taking risks.[5] In the case of drugs, when medical examiners are faced with uncertainty about the risks and benefits of a drug (as is usually the case), they tend to postpone the final decision and request more studies. Even when the public believes the system is too slow and retards the discovery of new medicines, the debate bogs down in details about how to write better regulations or get better regulators.[6] The debate loses sight of Adam Smith's basic point about the efficiency of the marketplace. Missing is any real consideration of how incentives in a private market might be substituted for regulations, perhaps through the use of stricter liability laws or of private testing and certification laboratories as alternatives to FDA regulation. The more we learn about the shortcomings of regulatory bodies, the greater our incentive to return the regulatory reform debate to these fundamental questions about market alternatives.

Not all of the authors in this volume agree with this interpretation. Still, the analyses and the information in the papers and commentaries reported here do help us to understand how international drug markets work and how the pattern of discovery, production, and trade is changing. If, by substituting market discipline for regulation, we can increase the production of new and safer drugs, increase the safety of old drugs, and allow a freer flow of drugs and information to world markets, we can hasten the day when the promise of modern medicine is extended to more of the world's population.

ROBERT B. HELMS
Director
Center for Health Policy Research
American Enterprise Institute

---

[5] See, for example, Sam Peltzman, *Regulation of Pharmaceutical Innovation* (Washington, D.C.: American Enterprise Institute, 1974); and William A. Niskanen, Jr., *Bureaucracy and Representative Government* (Chicago: Aldine, Atherton, Inc., 1971).

[6] For a recent discussion of the incentives influencing the behavior of bureaucrats and why the substitution of "more intelligent" or "more efficient" people will not likely lead to an improvement in social policy, see Thomas Sowell, *Knowledge and Decisions* (New York: Basic Books, Inc., 1980), pp. 140–149, especially p. 147.

Part One

The Multinational Pharmaceutical Industry: Evidence of Product Diffusion and Technology Transfer

Introduction

Rachel McCulloch

My area of expertise is international trade and investment policy in general, rather than the pharmaceutical industry in particular. My introductory remarks therefore will relate the two papers in this session to the overall picture of foreign trade and technology transfer in R&D-intensive industries and will indicate the important ways in which pharmaceuticals *differ* from the typical pattern.

High-technology industries have played a prominent role in recent U.S. trade performance. At the same time that much of U.S. manufacturing has moved into deep trade deficit, the high-technology industries have continued to achieve record trade surpluses. Nevertheless, there has been a great deal of concern that the U.S. commercial advantage in these industries will be eroded through the transfer of advanced technology abroad. That concern is reflected in Professor Brada's paper for this session. However, international technology transfer is not an isolated phenomenon: it must be seen as an integral part of the overall development and commercial exploitation of new technology.

The *trade product cycle* hypothesis suggests that the United States, with its giant scientific and technological establishment, but with relatively high production costs in manufacturing, is likely to be most competitive internationally when supplying new or unique products. In the typical pattern, as these products become firmly established in the U.S. domestic market, multinational enterprises start to serve markets abroad through exports. But at this point, the U.S. technological lead and the U.S. market share may begin to be eroded by foreign competition. As volume grows, imitators appear, prices tend to fall, and production costs, tariffs, and taxes become increasingly important. Standardization may facilitate the substitution of relatively unskilled labor for other inputs. Foreign production facilities often will be established, and, if the cost advantage of these foreign facilities is decisive, the U.S. market itself may also be served by imports, which displace competing U.S. production.

The trade product cycle hypothesis thus suggests that for any new product or process, comparative advantage will, over time, tend to shift

3

from the United States to other nations—either to other industrialized nations or, with some simpler manufactures, to developing nations. It also suggests that the attractiveness of R&D investments by multinational corporations depends in part on the opportunities to profit at some stage in the process by transferring the fruits of R&D abroad. Professor Brada points out the importance of certain U.S. and foreign government trade restrictions and tax policies in influencing the nature and the timing of technology transfer in pharmaceuticals.

Professor Grabowski's paper highlights a somewhat different aspect of the international diffusion of new products. Pharmaceuticals are unique in the long and costly procedure required before a new product can be sold in a given national market. If this process is, for whatever reasons, more costly (relative to expected benefits) in the United States than in other developed nations, U.S. innovators may well choose to introduce their new drugs abroad, thus producing the "drug lag" in U.S. introductions. The extent to which this lag results from stringent government regulation alone, rather than from a combination of other factors, is less clear. The Brada and Grabowski papers together suggest that some bulk production that might otherwise take place in the United States takes place abroad because of the interaction of two features of current U.S. policy toward pharmaceuticals, namely, slower regulatory approval of new drugs and prohibition of exports of bulk or dosage forms of non-approved drugs.

The two papers in this session draw on very different kinds of evidence. Brada's data come almost exclusively from interviews with managers of multinational drug firms. Although these informants are obviously knowledgeable, their responses may take account of potentially profitable feedback from the opinions expressed. Grabowski's regression analysis focuses upon quantitative variables and, in particular, one that he calls "regulatory stringency." As he indicates, however, the measure actually used could reflect other factors as well, so that the regression results must be interpreted with care.

Regulation and the International Diffusion of Pharmaceuticals

Henry G. Grabowski

Several recent analyses of the pharmaceutical industry have examined whether a "drug lag" exists between the United States and other developed countries. William Wardell, a clinical pharmacologist, first investigated this issue in a series of papers comparing the availability and introduction dates of new chemical entities (NCEs) in the United States and Great Britain for several major therapeutic classes of drugs. He concluded that a drug lag in U.S. NCE introductions has characterized the period since the 1962 Kefauver amendment and further that this lag has involved medically important drug therapies. His most recent work indicates that this drug lag may have lessened but not disappeared during the last few years.[1]

The notion of a drug lag, advanced by Wardell and others, has been vigorously disputed by successive groups of top Food and Drug Administration officials. Donald Kennedy, while serving as FDA Commissioner, wrote an article in the *Journal of the American Medical Association* criticizing this notion.[2] In particular, he sets forth two basic objections to the concept of a drug lag and the implied role of FDA regulation in causing such a lag. First, Dr. Kennedy argues that it is important to focus on the *quality* of new drugs available here or abroad and not their *quantity*. Second, he argues that the general pattern of drug introductions across countries does not support the hypothesis that drug lag is unique to the U.S. situation or is primarily caused by regulation here. Specifically, he argues that there is great variability in the pattern of introductions across countries, with some countries lead-

---

[1] Wardell's earlier studies of the drug lag issue are presented in chapters 6 through 10 of William Wardell and Louis Lasagna, *Regulation and Drug Development* (Washington: American Enterprise Institute for Public Policy Research, 1975). His analysis has recently been updated in William M. Wardell, "The Drug Lag Revisited: Comparison by Therapeutic Areas of Patterns of Drugs Marketed in the United States and in Great Britain from 1972 through 1976," *Clinical and Pharmacological Therapy*, vol. 24 (November 1978), pp. 499–524.

[2] Donald Kennedy, "A Calm Look at 'Drug Lag,'" *Journal of the American Medical Association*, vol. 239 (January 30, 1978), pp. 423–426.

ing in some drugs and therapeutic areas and lagging in others. This variability suggests a greater importance for nonregulatory factors (such as differences in medical needs and practices or general economic considerations) than for regulatory factors in determining where drugs are first introduced and how they are diffused across countries.[3]

In an earlier paper,[4] John Vernon and I analyzed the introduction of U.S.-discovered drugs into the United Kingdom for the period from 1960 to 1972 to see how increased regulatory controls in this country after 1962 might be influencing the decisions of U.S. multinational firms on foreign introductions. Our results do shed some light on the second basic point raised by Commissioner Kennedy. In particular, we found that in the early 1960s, the vast majority of U.S.-discovered NCEs were introduced into the United Kingdom only after first becoming available in this country, but a dramatic shift in this situation has occurred over time. By the final subperiod that we analyzed (1972–1974), more than two-thirds of U.S.-discovered NCEs introduced in the United Kingdom were either introduced later here or have not yet become available in the United States at all. This dramatic shift suggests that regulatory differences across countries have had an important effect on where new drugs are first introduced and on the lags in introductions across countries. It would be difficult to explain this shift in U.S. firm behavior on other grounds.

This paper expands on earlier analysis. In particular, it focuses on the time pattern of U.S. and foreign introductions for all NCEs introduced into the United States during the period 1963 to 1975. Using this population, I analyze the general pattern of leads and lags between the United States and three European countries—the United Kingdom, (West) Germany, and France. The choice of these countries was dictated largely by the availability of data, but they nevertheless provide an interesting set of countries for such an analysis. In addition, in the case of the United Kingdom, I was able to obtain sufficiently detailed information to undertake a regression analysis relating the length of the lag between U.S. and U.K. introductions to various regulatory and non-

---

[3] See, however, Professor Wardell's response to this "asynchrony argument" on drug introductions across countries in William Wardell, "A Close Inspection of the 'Calm Look,'" *Journal of the American Medical Association*, vol. 239 (May 12, 1978), pp. 2004–2011. Professor Wardell points out that, although drug introductions do show a great deal of variability across countries, the data used by Dr. Kennedy imply a systematic lag in U.S. introductions, compared with those in other developed countries.

[4] Henry G. Grabowski and John M. Vernon, "Consumer Protection Regulation in Ethical Drugs," *American Economic Review*, vol. 67 (February 1977), pp. 359–364.

regulatory variables. This latter analysis is only in a preliminary stage, but some interesting findings have emerged in the first pass through the data. These are reported here.

In addition, this study addresses two general questions not considered in my earlier analysis. The first is the question of drug quality raised by Commissioner Kennedy and others. Specifically, I use the FDA's own classification of drugs according to whether the NCE provides an important, a modest, or no therapeutic gain over existing therapies to see whether there are significant differences between the lag for drugs ranked as important and the lag for other drugs. The second question is the effect of FDA regulation on the introduction lag of foreign-discovered drugs into the United States—a question of increased importance because foreign-discovered drugs now account for a sizeable portion of U.S. NCE introductions (more than 40 percent), yet the average introduction lag for them is several years longer than for U.S.-discovered drugs. It is appropriate to inquire how much of this is due to regulatory factors.

Before we turn to the discussion of the characteristics of the sample and the empirical results, it is worth assembling some background information on regulatory conditions and other relevant factors in the four countries.

Background

Characteristics of Regulation in the United States. Regulatory controls over new pharmaceuticals began much earlier in the United States than in Europe, and the controls here consistently have been more stringent in scope and intensity than those abroad. Premarket reviews of drug safety by the FDA began in 1938 with the passage of the Food, Drug, and Cosmetic Act. In 1962, the Kefauver-Harris amendments, passed in the wake of the thalidomide disaster in Europe, extended FDA controls in two important ways. First, they required that new drugs, before they could be marketed, be proven effective as well as safe for their intended use, and they stipulated that the standard of scientific evidence acceptable for demonstrating effectiveness be "adequate and well controlled investigations, including clinical investigations, conducted by experts." This latter requirement (in the way it has been administered by the FDA) is generally regarded as a major factor in producing much longer and costlier development periods for new drugs in the post-1962 period. Second, the 1962 amendments instituted FDA controls over clinical testing on human subjects, requiring firms to submit a new drug investigational plan (IND) prior to clinical testing.

7

In addition, the FDA was given a supervisory role over the clinical development process with the authority to delay or halt testing as new clinical test data accumulated on drug toxicity and efficacy.

Various studies have documented the fact that the economics of new drug development and introduction changed dramatically after 1962.[5] In the early 1960s, a new chemical entity took about three to four years to develop (on average) and required a few million dollars in total R&D costs. By the middle 1970s, development times were seven to ten years; the time necessary to obtain FDA approval of a new drug application alone takes two years (on average). In addition, studies suggest that the average cost of developing an NCE has increased many times. A recent study by Ronald Hansen of the University of Rochester estimated this cost at more than $50 million.[6] Not all the cost increase can be attributed to regulatory factors, but a comparative international study by John Vernon, Lacy Thomas, and me indicates that regulation has been one of the major factors increasing R&D costs.[7]

Before we turn to the discussion of regulatory requirements in Europe, one further aspect of U.S. regulatory development is worth emphasizing: U.S. policy toward foreign clinical trials. Until very recently, the FDA did not accept data from foreign clincial trials as evidence in support of claims on a drug's safety or efficacy. The FDA argued it was not in a position to monitor the quality of data collected by foreign investigators to the same extent as for data collected by U.S. investigators. Hence, it required drugs developed abroad to undergo substantial duplicate testing in this country before they were eligible for marketing. As will be shown later, this policy seems to have had a significant effect in delaying the introduction of foreign-discovered drugs into the United States—even those foreign drugs that represent significant advances.

---

[5] For a survey of various studies, see chapters 2 and 3 of Henry Grabowski, *Drug Regulation and Innovation: Empirical Evidence and Policy Options* (Washington: American Enterprise Institute for Public Policy Research, 1976).

[6] Ronald W. Hansen, "The Pharmaceutical Development Process: Estimates of Current Development Costs and Times and the Effects of Regulatory Changes," in R. I. Chien, ed., *Issues in Pharmaceutical Economics* (Cambridge: Ballinger, 1979), chapter 11. A very detailed study of development and regulatory approval times on which the Hansen study draws is W. M. Wardell, M. Hassar, S. Anavekar, and L. Lasagna, "The Rate of Development of New Drugs in the United States, 1963 through 1975," in *Clinical Pharmacology and Therapeutics*, vol. 24 (August 1978), p. 133.

[7] Henry G. Grabowski, John M. Vernon, and Lacy G. Thomas, "Estimating the Effects of Regulation on Innovation: An International Comparative Analysis of the Pharmaceutical Industry," *Journal of Law and Economics*, vol. 21, no. 1 (April 1978), pp. 133–163.

8

Regulation in Europe. Premarket drug regulation and approval did not come into existence in the three European countries until after 1962, with the thalidomide experience the main factor triggering a change in European practices. All three countries now have organizational counterparts to the FDA and premarket approval requirements for pharmaceuticals.

Of the European countries under study, the United Kingdom is generally regarded as having regulatory standards most comparable to those of the United States in depth and quality of the review process. Premarket approval of pharmaceuticals there began in 1963.[8] The United Kingdom also requires prior authorization of clinical testing on patients based on the submission of preclinical animal tests and research protocol as in the United States.

Important differences in "regulatory philosophy" between the two countries have been pointed out in literature by Wardell and Lasagna, Dunlop, and others.[9] First, the United Kingdom places much greater emphasis on safety than on efficacy. Although the efficacy of a drug is considered in assessing its risks and benefits, the U.K. authorities do not require the same elaborate testing and documentation to establish efficacy that is required by the FDA. Second, the U.K. system relies more on outside committees of scientific and medical experts to evaluate drug safety and efficacy and as a consequence has been characterized as less bureaucratic and adversarial than the U.S. system, which relies for the most part on civil servants. Finally, the United Kingdom historically has had a more tolerant attitude toward foreign trials, taking the position that the quality of the study is controlling, not the location or nationality of its investigator.

France and West Germany also instituted premarket reviews of safety and efficacy data in the post-1962 period—France in 1965 and West Germany in 1971. A recent FDA evaluation categorized the regulatory systems in these two countries as less strict than those of the United States or United Kingdom in the depth of their review processes and the

---

[8] The Committee on the Safety of Drugs was appointed for this purpose by the Minister of Health in 1964 and actually operated on a voluntary basis (with apparently 100 percent compliance) until the Medicines Act became operative in 1971. At that time the committee was renamed the Committee on the Safety of Medicines and received full statutory powers. For a further discussion of the British regulatory system, see Sir Derrick Dunlop, "The British System of Drug Regulation," in R. L. Landau, ed., *Regulating New Drugs* (Chicago: University of Chicago Center for Policy Study, 1973), pp. 230–242.

[9] Wardell and Lasagna, *Regulation and Drug Development*; and Dunlop, "The British System of Drug Regulation."

TABLE 1

ESTIMATED WORLD PHARMACEUTICAL SALES
BY COUNTRY AND MARKET-SHARE RANK, 1973

Country	Rank	Estimated 1973 Sales (millions of U.S. dollars)
United States	1	5,500
Japan	2	4,100
West Germany	3	2,000
France	4	1,800
Italy	5	1,560
Spain	6	725
United Kingdom	7	700
Total world sales		27,180

SOURCE: Barrie G. James, *The Future of the Multinational Pharmaceutical Industry to 1990* (New York: Halstead Press, 1977).

evidence necessary for approval.[10] It is also true that neither of these countries requires the prior authorization of clinical trials (that is, the IND procedure) that is required in the United States and United Kingdom.

One further point to be noted is the French policy toward foreign clinical trials. France generally does not accept foreign data as the sole basis for drug approval, which means that some duplicative testing is normally required for a drug to receive regulatory approval.[11] This policy can result in regulatory lags in the introduction of foreign-discovered drugs into France, even if they originate in countries with stricter overall reviews of safety and efficacy. We will consider this point further during the empirical analysis.

Market Size and Economic Factors. In this section, I briefly consider some of the economic factors—such as market size and drug prices—

---

[10] See Chart 1 in Table C of the study by the Food and Drug Administration, "Impact of Disclosure of Safety and Efficacy Data on Expenditures for Pharmaceutical Research and Development," mimeographed, Washington, D.C., 1978. This study was done in compliance with executive orders 11821 and 11929, which require federal agencies to make economic analyses of legislative proposals to Congress—in this instance the Drug Regulation Reform Act of 1978.

[11] For a description of this and other French regulations, see the discussion in David A. Kay, *The International Regulation of Pharmaceutical Drugs* (Washington, D.C.: American Society of International Law, 1976).

that can have a significant bearing on the rapidity of drug diffusion across countries.

Table 1 presents data estimates on the market for pharmaceuticals for each country in 1973 dollars. All four countries considered here are among the top ten markets for pharmaceuticals, with the U.S. market about eight times the size of the U.K. market and the West German and French markets in between.

Table 2 presents data estimates on the domestic and foreign market shares in each of the four countries for 1973. The United States market had the least penetration by foreign rivals (which achieved only 16 percent of total sales), while the United Kingdom was the country most open to foreign competition, with foreign firms accounting for 63 percent of the market (and U.S. firms, in particular, capturing 38 percent). France and West Germany more closely resemble the United States, with domestic firms capturing more than 60 percent of the market in each country.

The stronger market performance of U.S. firms in the United Kingdom (as against U.S. market share in France or West Germany) has been attributed to several causes including greater similarities in medical training and practices between the United States and United Kingdom, stronger historical and cultural links between these two "Anglo" nations, and U.K. government policy that is more liberal toward U.S. competition

TABLE 2

ESTIMATED DOMESTIC U.S. AND OTHER FOREIGN MARKET SHARES IN PHARMACEUTICALS FOR THE UNITED STATES, WEST GERMANY, FRANCE, AND UNITED KINGDOM, 1973

(percent)

Country	Domestic Firms' Share	U.S. Firms' Share	Other Foreign Firms' Share	Total
United States	84.0	—	16.0	100
West Germany	70.3	12.6	17.1	100
France	62.2	17.4	20.4	100
United Kingdom	36.3	38.4	25.3	100

SOURCE: James, *Future of the Multinational Pharmaceutical Industry.*

than West German or French government policy.[12] In any event, the much larger market shares that U.S. firms achieve in the United Kingdom than in the other countries counterbalance the lower overall U.K. market size so that U.S. firms' sales are roughly equal in value in all three countries (ranging between $250 and $300 million).

Some comparative studies of drug prices in Europe have also been performed by Michael Cooper among others.[13] In particular, Cooper finds drug prices in Europe are highest in West Germany and lowest in France. The former result is not surprising, given that West Germany is the only one of these three European countries without formal government price controls on drugs. Cooper's results indicate that the French price controls, which set prices for each individual drug on a cost formula basis, have apparently had a more severe effect on prices than the price controls in the United Kingdom, where target profit rates are negotiated with each company and actual price formation left up to the individual companies.

To sum up the main points emerging from this brief review, comparative price studies suggest that profit margins on pharmaceuticals have been greatest in West Germany and lowest in France, and market share data suggest that market entry conditions for foreign firms (particularly U.S. firms) have been most favorable in the United Kingdom. Although these general observations do not give rise to "hard" predictions concerning the expected rate of international diffusion or drug lags between countries, they are worth keeping in mind when we interpret the results presented in the next section.

Empirical Analysis

Basic Characteristics of the Data Samples. As we noted in the introductory section, the basic sample being analyzed is made up of all new chemical entities (NCEs) introduced into the United States from 1963 to 1975. The definition of NCE used here excludes salts and esters of previously marketed drugs as well as combinations or new dosage forms of existing products. Figure 1 shows a time plot of U.S. NCE introductions from 1963 through 1975. The average number of NCEs introduced over this period was thirteen a year, with considerable year-to-year fluctuation, but no distinct trend.

---

[12] See, in particular, some of the general discussion on these matters in Barrie G. James, *The Future of the Multinational Pharmaceutical Industry to 1990* (New York: Halstead Press, 1977).

[13] Michael Cooper, *European Pharmaceutical Prices 1964–74* (London: Croom Helm, 1976).

FIGURE 1

U.S. NCE INTRODUCTIONS, BY YEAR

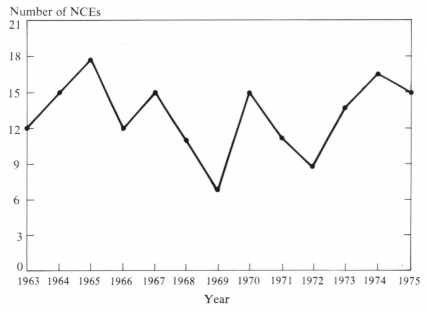

Table 3 shows some basic information on the national origin of NCE introductions during this period. The first column of this table defines national origin on the basis of the location of the R&D laboratory that discovered each of the NCEs. These data were initially obtained from the publications of Paul deHaen.[14] Under this definition, U.S. research laboratories accounted for 59 percent of total introductions over the period with all but a few of these coming from the private pharmaceutical industry. The United Kingdom accounted for the largest number of foreign-discovered introductions (11 percent) followed by Switzerland, West Germany, Japan, and a number of countries (including France) with five or fewer drugs.

The second way national origin is defined in Table 3 is according to the country where the discovering firm is owned. Thus, if a foreign

---

[14] Paul deHaen, "New Single Drugs Marketed in England, France, Germany, and Italy, 1960 to 1965," mimeographed, February 1973 (distributed by Paul deHaen, Inc.), and *New Drug Analysis, Europe* (New York: Paul deHaen, Inc.), various volumes, 1967–1976. These data from deHaen were checked using a variety of sources, and some introduction dates were modified on the basis of alternate data (including marketing information from IMS America and survey response data privately supplied by Professor William Wardell on U.S. and U.K. entry dates).

13

TABLE 3

U.S. NCEs Introduced, by Country of Origin, 1963–1975

Country	Number (Percent) of NCEs Discovered[a]	Number (Percent) of NCEs Discovered[b]
United States	99.5	87.5
	(59)	(52)
United Kingdom	18.5	22.5
	(11)	(13)
Switzerland	9.5	18.5
	(6)	(11)
West Germany	7.0	7.0
	(4)	(4)
Japan	6.0	6.0
	(4)	(4)
Others	28.5	26.5
	(17)	(16)
Total	169	169
	(100)	(100)

NOTE: Duplicate sources of discoveries are assigned a value of 0.5 on this table.
[a] Based on the country where R&D was performed that first discovered drug's pharmacological action.
[b] Based on the nationality of parent firm sponsoring the research that first discovered the drug.
SOURCE: Paul deHaen, Inc., various publications. See footnote 14.

subsidiary of a multinational firm discovers a new drug, that drug is assigned to the country of the parent firm. This method of defining national origin significantly increases the percentage of NCEs attributed to Switzerland, reflecting the fact that a number of NCEs were discovered in the U.S. research labs of Swiss firms (Hoffman-LaRoche, in particular) during this period. Aside from this change, there is little difference between the two classifications. Under both definitions, the United Kingdom and Switzerland are the leading foreign sources of NCE introductions in the United States, followed by West Germany and Japan.

In most of the analysis that follows, when the term "U.S.-discovered drug" or "foreign-discovered drug" is used, the definition is based on the location of the R&D laboratory rather than the nationality of the parent firm. For reasons that will become apparent later, the former is the more relevant concept when we are dealing with effects of regula-

FIGURE 2

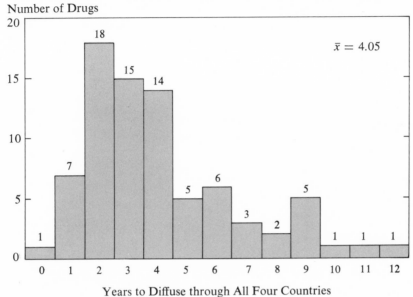

DISTRIBUTION OF DIFFUSION TIMES THROUGH ALL FOUR COUNTRIES

Number of Drugs

$\bar{x} = 4.05$

Years to Diffuse through All Four Countries

tion on the diffusion of pharmaceuticals, although using the other definition would rarely change the results in a material way because only a handful of drugs are affected.

Table 4 provides some basic information on the extent of the diffusion of this sample of NCEs across the three countries in Europe under study here. The table shows that 81 NCEs (or nearly half the total sample of 169 NCEs) were introduced in all three, while 26 NCEs (15 percent of the sample) were not introduced in *any* of the three. When the United States is paired directly with each country, the United Kingdom had the greatest number of common introductions with the United States (77 percent) followed by West Germany (70 percent) and France (56 percent).[15]

Figure 2 provides a bar graph showing the distribution of times required for NCE diffusion from the first country of introduction to the last for the drugs that were introduced into all four countries. The mean time for this diffusion process was approximately four years.

---

[15] Since my data on NCE introductions in Europe (but not in the United States), are spotty for years prior to 1960, there is the possibility of some downward bias in the estimated number of common NCE introductions.

15

TABLE 4

Diffusion of U.S. NCE Introductions through Europe: All U.S. NCEs Introduced, 1963–1975

Sample	Total NCEs	Number (Percent) Introduced In:				
		All three European countries	Two of three European countries	One of three European countries	Only United States
All United States NCE introductions	169 (100)	81 (48)	34 (20)	28 (17)	26 (15)
All U.S. NCE introductions classified as important therapeutic advances by FDA[a]	42 (100)	28 (67)	5 (12)	8 (19)	1 (2)
All U.S. NCE introductions achieving sales in excess of $10 million in U.S. over first three years after introduction[b]	53 (100)	37 (70)	12 (23)	4 (7)	0 (0)

[a] FDA classification of significant drugs released by Commissioner Schmidt in congressional testimony only covers the period 1950–1973. See footnote 16.
[b] Sales data were obtained from IMS America.
Source: See footnote 14.

However, there is considerable variance in this statistic with a few drugs taking a full decade or more to diffuse across all four countries.

As one might expect, both the length of time and the extent of diffusion will be influenced by the medical and economic significance of the NCE. In row two of Table 4, the extent of diffusion through Europe is displayed for those U.S. NCE introductions classified by FDA as important therapeutic advances.[16] Two-thirds of these drugs were introduced in all three European countries, and the mean time for complete diffusion across the four countries was reduced slightly (to 3.8 years) from the diffusion time for the larger sample (4.05 years). The third row shows those U.S. NCE introductions achieving cumulative sales of $10 million or more during the first three years after their introduction. This was accomplished by fifty-three drugs or about 30 percent of the total sample. Of these drugs, 70 percent diffused across all three European countries, and the mean time for complete diffusion was three years, or nearly a full year less than for the larger sample considered in Figure 2.

In sum, there is clearly a great deal of commonality of NCEs introduced here and those introduced in these major European markets. This is what one would predict for drugs that have all cleared the very stringent regulatory hurdles provided by the FDA. At the same time, there are also many drugs (particularly those with smaller sales or possessing lesser therapeutic significance) that have not become available in one or more of these three European countries. There are also, of course, many drugs introduced in Europe that do not become available here.[17]

Leads and Lags in NCE Introductions between the U.S. and Europe.
This section presents an initial analysis of the main question of interest in the current paper, namely, the time pattern of leads and lags in NCE introductions in the United States and each of the three European countries.

Table 5 provides some summary data on the time pattern of leads

---

[16] These FDA classifications were obtained from the appendix to FDA Commissioner Schmidt, "Testimony before U.S. Senate Subcommittee on Health, August 16, 1974," in U.S. Congress, Senate, Subcommittee on Health of the Committee on Labor and Public Welfare, *Hearings on Legislation Amending the Public Health Service Act and the Federal Food, Drug, and Cosmetic Act*, 93rd Congress, August 1974, pp. 30–49.

[17] In this regard, William Wardell estimated there were roughly 50 percent more total NCE introductions for the United Kingdom than for the United States in the 1962–1971 time period. See Wardell and Lasagna, *Regulation and Drug Development*, chapter 7.

TABLE 5

NCE Introduction Dates, United States Compared with United Kingdom, France, and West Germany: All U.S. NCE Introductions, 1963–1975

Number (Percent) of Common NCEs Introduced

Country	Total	Before United States	Same year	After United States	Not Introduced
United Kingdom	130 (100)	69 (53)	27 (21)	34 (26)	39
West Germany	112 (100)	58 (52)	26 (23)	28 (25)	57
France	94 (100)	35 (37)	12 (13)	47 (50)	75
Three European countries combined[a]	143 (100)	84 (59)	29 (20)	30 (21)	26

[a] In this case, the U.S. introduction data is compared with earliest date of introduction for the three European countries.
Source: See footnote 14.

and lags for those NCEs that were introduced in both countries of each of these country pairs. This table shows a considerable drug lag between the United States and the United Kingdom, as well as between the United States and Germany—that is, significantly more of the NCEs that are eventually available in both countries become available in the United States second. On the other hand, there appears to be no comparable drug lag from France to the United States. A greater number of the mutually available NCEs were introduced first in the United States than in France (forty-seven NCEs as against thirty-five NCEs). In addition, the number of U.S. NCEs not available in France (the last column of Table 5) was much greater than the number not available in the United Kingdom or Germany.

The final row of Table 5 analyzes the leads and lags between the U.S. introduction and the earliest introduction in one of these three countries. These data show almost three times as many NCEs were introduced in Europe first (that is, in the United Kingdom, Germany, or France) as in this country. This is true despite the fact that the majority of these U.S. NCE introductions were discovered in a U.S. research laboratory (Table 3).

Table 5 provides an aggregate picture of the pattern of NCE introductions for the 1963-to-1975 sample period. As such, it obscures some important differences across NCEs. Tables 6 through 8 show the time pattern of leads and lags with the NCEs broken down by U.S. or foreign origin. In addition, Tables 6 through 8 separate the data into two time periods (1963–1967 and 1968–1975).

Table 6 shows this information for the United Kingdom. One immediately obvious point is the difference in pattern between U.S.- and foreign-discovered drugs. The overwhelming majority of foreign-discovered NCEs were introduced abroad first. In particular, about nine in ten of the foreign-discovered NCEs were introduced in the United Kingdom either before or in the same year as in the United States. This pattern is also fairly stable across the two time periods shown in Table 6.

On the other hand, the observed pattern for U.S.-discovered NCEs changes significantly between the two periods. For the initial period (1963–1967), the number of mutual NCEs introduced first in the United States exceeds the comparable number for NCEs introduced first in the United Kingdom (seventeen NCEs in the former case to thirteen NCEs in the latter). However, the opposite is true for the second time period (1968–1975). There are almost twice as many U.S.-discovered NCEs in the United Kingdom before the United States as in the United States before the United Kingdom. Moreover, a perusal of the data for each individual year points to 1968 as a turning point in

TABLE 6

NCE Introductions, United States and United Kingdom, U.S. and Foreign Discoveries, 1963–1967 and 1968–1975

Period of Introduction in United States	Total	Number (Percent) of Common NCEs with United Kingdom Introduced			Not Introduced in United Kingdom
		Before United States	Same year	After United States	
U.S.-discovered NCEs					
1963–67	41 (100)	13 (32)	11 (27)	17 (41)	8
1968–75	37 (100)	18 (49)	8 (22)	11 (29)	16
Foreign-discovered NCEs					
1963–67	21 (100)	16 (76)	2 (10)	3 (14)	4
1968–75	36 (100)	27 (75)	6 (17)	3 (8)	11

NOTE: Five NCEs jointly discovered in the United States and abroad are included under both the U.S.- and foreign-discovered categories in tables 6 through 8.
SOURCE: See footnote 14.

the behavior of U.S. firms with regard to foreign introductions. In almost all years before 1968, the number of U.S.-discovered NCEs introduced in the United States before they were introduced in the United Kingdom exceeded those introduced in the United Kingdom first. After 1968, however, the reverse is true. Of course, I am focusing here only on mutual introductions and there are a number of NCEs introduced into one of these countries but not the other.

In addition to the trends displayed in Table 6, one can compute comparable trends in the length of the lags involved for each of the categories in this table. These data indicate an increasing lag between the United States and the United Kingdom for those mutual NCEs introduced in the United Kingdom first, and a decreasing lead for those NCEs introduced first in the United States (comparing the two time periods given in Table 6).[18] These data are therefore consistent with the basic pattern displayed in this table—an increasing tendency post-1962 for new drugs to become available in foreign countries first, regardless of the national origin of the NCE.

The analysis of U.S.-West German NCE introduction dates shown in Table 7 indicates a pattern almost identical to that for the United States and United Kingdom. The only difference between the two cases seems to be a somewhat greater tendency for more U.S.-discovered introductions to be marketed in the United Kingdom than in West Germany. This is consistent with the fact (see above) that U.S. firms generally have larger market shares in the United Kingdom than in West Germany.

Table 8, in turn, clearly implies that U.S.-discovered drugs generally have been introduced in France later than in the United Kingdom or Germany. Furthermore, a greater number of U.S.-discovered drugs were introduced in the United States before they were introduced in France in both periods, although the gap seems to narrow in the later period. As with the United Kingdom and West Germany, foreign-discovered NCEs were generally introduced in France before they were

---

[18] In particular, using the data on years of introduction presented in Table 6 from Paul deHaen, we find the average *lag* between the United States and the United Kingdom for *U.S.-discovered NCEs* introduced in the United Kingdom before the United States increased from 2.3 years in the first period to 4.5 years in the second period. At the same time, the average lead in *U.S.-discovered NCEs* introduced first in this country declined from 3.1 to 2.2 years between these two periods. Finally, the average lag for *foreign-discovered drugs* between the United States and the United Kingdom increased from 3.6 to 4.4 years over this period. The next section which provides an analysis of U.S.-U.K. data using a monthly "grid" on introduction dates for these two countries shows similar trends.

21

TABLE 7

NCE Introductions, United States and West Germany, U.S. and Foreign Discoveries, 1963–1967 and 1968–1975

Number (Percent) of Common NCEs with Germany Introduced

Period of Introduction in United States	Total	Before United States	Same year	After United States	Not Introduced in Germany
U.S.-discovered NCEs					
1963–1967	33	9	11	13	16
	(100)	(27)	(34)	(39)	
1968–1975	31	15	6	10	22
	(100)	(48)	(19)	(32)	
Foreign-discovered NCEs					
1963–1967	15	13	1	1	10
	(100)	(86)	(7)	(7)	
1968–1975	38	24	10	4	9
	(100)	(63)	(26)	(11)	

SOURCE: See footnote 14.

TABLE 8

NCE INTRODUCTIONS, UNITED STATES AND FRANCE, U.S. AND FOREIGN DISCOVERIES, 1963–1967 AND 1968–1975

Period of Introduction in United States	Total	Number (Percent) of Common NCEs with France Introduced			
		Before United States	Same year	After United States	Not Introduced in France
U.S.-discovered NCEs					
1963–1967	28	3	3	22	21
	(100)	(11)	(11)	(78)	
1968–1975	24	7	5	12	29
	(100)	(29)	(21)	(50)	
Foreign-discovered NCEs					
1963–1967	14	8	1	5	11
	(100)	(57)	(7)	(36)	
1968–1975	33	19	4	10	14
	(100)	(58)	(12)	(30)	

SOURCE: See footnote 14.

introduced in the United States. However, the differences are much less dramatic than for the United Kingdom or West Germany.

The tendency for U.S.-discovered drugs to be introduced later in France than the United Kingdom and West Germany probably reflects both regulatory and economic factors previously discussed in the background section. In particular, although the French regulatory standards are not as stringent as those in the United Kingdom or United States, France does require that *some* clinical testing be done within that country, which slows down the introduction process—and, in addition, as we noted above, price controls on drugs in France have been more severe than elsewhere in Europe.

The results in Tables 6 through 8 are consistent with my earlier analysis (with John Vernon) of the timing of U.S.-discovered drugs in the United Kingdom.[19] In particular, we found that before 1962, U.S.-discovered drugs were almost always introduced first in the United States, but this pattern gradually shifted over the post-1962 period as U.S. regulatory standards increased in stringency relative to those of other countries. By the early 1970s, the majority of U.S.-discovered drugs introduced in the United Kingdom were available there before they were available in the United States.

The analysis here, where drugs are classified according to their U.S. introduction dates, reveals a similar pattern. In particular, the first five years after 1962 can be interpreted as a period of adjustment to the more stringent regulatory conditions evolving from the Kefauver-Harris Amendments. Both the cost of developing and the time taken to develop and introduce NCEs into the United States increased rapidly, and as firms became more cognizant of this fact, they responded by introducing their NCEs in foreign countries before they introduced them in the United States. The introduction pattern for both the United Kingdom and Germany is consistent with this interpretation. By the end of the 1960s, this adjustment process had apparently reached the point where the majority of U.S.-discovered NCEs were being introduced in these foreign countries before the United States.

The data on the introduction of foreign-discovered drugs into the United States are also interesting and instructive. I have concentrated my attention thus far on the time pattern of NCEs originating in the United States, but there is at least some evidence from our analysis that the introduction lag of foreign-discovered drugs was also increasing over the post-1962 period. This point will be considered in further detail in what follows. The analysis below suggests that this component of the drug

---

[19] Grabowski and Vernon, "Consumer Protection Regulation," pp. 362–363.

lag may have been one of the more important effects of regulation in its impact on the availability of significant new medicines.

A Regression Analysis of the United States-United Kingdom Drug Lag. In order to gain further insight into the role of regulation in causing these NCE introduction lags, I carried out a regression analysis restricted (largely because of data availability) to the United States and United Kingdom. In particular, I was able to obtain for the United Kingdom the exact month of introduction for most drugs in the sample,[20] and this information was also available for the United States from the publications of Paul deHaen. Hence, I could calculate (or at least approximate) the size of the lag (or lead) in months between the United States and the United Kingdom. This lag variable was calculated for all the NCEs mutually introduced into the two countries. Although the choice of the U.S.-U.K. country pair was made largely because of data availability, an analysis of these countries would be of particular interest in any case— the links between them being generally stronger than those between the United States and the other two countries. It is hoped that more detailed introduction data on Germany and France will become available in the near future, but what we have here is probably the most interesting comparison.

In analyzing introduction lags, it is important to bear in mind the different stages of the innovational process through which a new drug entity passes. These are (1) synthesis of a new entity and preclinical testing in animals, (2) clinical testing in humans under the general supervision of regulatory officials, (3) submission of safety and efficacy test results to regulatory officials for approval, and (4) commercialization after regulatory approval.

The regulatory policy and procedures of a country influence the time any NCE spends in the development and regulatory-approval stages. In particular, as a country's regulatory standards become more stringent and comprehensive in character, the number of tests in the preclinical and clinical development periods increases, and so do the cost and time required to perform these tests. In addition, the efficiency of a country's regulatory officials in monitoring the development process

---

[20] These data are based on *Monthly Index of Medical Specialties* (MIMS) as presented in Arthur W. Lake, "Foreign Competition and the U.K. Pharmaceutical Industry," National Bureau of Economic Research Working Paper No. 155, New York, N.Y., November 1976. Some of these data were also obtained from private company sources. In the case of missing observations, I approximated the U.K. month of introduction by using the month of June as the entry date rather than discarding the observations.

and approving new drug applications after safety and efficacy tests have been completed will influence the total gestation period for a new drug and, correspondingly, its time of introduction there relative to other countries. The time of introduction also, of course, will be influenced by nonregulatory delays in performing required tests or in the filing of the new drug application with regulatory authorities.

In developing hypotheses, it is analytically useful to decompose the total lag in a new drug's introduction into the United States and the United Kingdom into the following three components:

(1) $$LAG_i = LD_i + LA_i + LF_i,$$

where

> $LAG_i =$ the total lag ($+$ or $-$) in months between the time of introduction in the United Kingdom and United States of the ith NCE,
>
> $LD_i =$ lag due to differences in clinical development time necessary to meet regulatory standards in the United States versus the United Kingdom for the ith NCE,
>
> $LA_i =$ lag due to differences in regulatory approval time for the ith NCE in the United States versus the United Kingdom, and
>
> $LF_i =$ any other time lags arising from delays in filing applications or initiating required testing in the United States versus the United Kingdom.

We shall proceed analytically by developing hypotheses about the factors that influence each of the three components of the total lag. These will then be combined into a single regression equation model for statistical estimation.

In the case of the first lag component, LD_i, the following structure is hypothesized:

$$\overset{(+)\quad(-)\quad(-)}{}$$
(2) $$LD_i = f(FOR_i, RANK_i, MKT_i),$$

or in linear form,

(2a) $$LD_i = \alpha_0 + \alpha_1 FOR_i + \alpha_2\, RANK_i + \alpha_3 MKT_i + u_{i1},$$

with $\alpha_1 > 0, \alpha_2 < 0, \alpha_3 > 0,$

where

> $FOR_i =$ a dummy variable taking on the value 1 if the ith NCE is of foreign origin and 0 otherwise,

$RANK_i = $ a dummy variable taking the value 1 if the FDA has ranked the ith NCE as an important therapeutic advance and 0 otherwise,

$MKT_i = $ a dummy variable taking on the value 1 if the ith NCE achieved \$10 million in sales during its first three years after introduction and 0 otherwise, and

$u_{i1} = $ a random error term.

The first variable included is a dummy variable *FOR* for those NCEs originating in foreign countries. As noted above, the FDA has historically not accepted foreign trials as sufficient evidence for new drug application (NDA) approval, so that foreign-discovered drugs have had to undergo duplicate clinical testing in this country. This tends to increase the total development period lag for foreign-discovered and foreign-developed drugs relative to those emanating from this country.

Second, the dummy variable *RANK* is included for those NCEs the FDA ranks as important therapeutic advances. As I noted at the outset, the FDA frequently has maintained that the drug lag is primarily confined to drugs with little or no important therapeutic gain. If the FDA put "important" drugs on a faster regulatory track, one might expect to observe significantly shorter (or nonexistent) lags for drugs ranked as important gains by the FDA than for the sample as a whole. The inclusion of the *RANK* variable is designed to test this hypothesis.

Third, the variable *MKT* is included as a measure of the economic significance of a new drug entity.[21] To the extent that a new drug has a large potential market and expected profits in this country, the firm has added incentives to reduce the longer expected development time here by incurring extra costs (through parallel tests, for example). This is subject, of course, to FDA regulatory constraints on the development process, but it is reasonable to hypothesize some flexibility in this regard.

The second component of the overall lag, LA_i, encompasses the differences in time for regulatory officials to approve new drug entity applications in the United States versus the United Kingdom. I was able to obtain from FDA files the regulatory approval time for each NCE in our sample (that is, the length of time from first NDA submission to FDA approval). No corresponding data were available on the United Kingdom. Nevertheless, one may postulate a linear relation between

---

[21] As can be seen from the data in the first column of Table 4, approximately one-third of the NCEs in our sample had sales during the first three years after introduction of more than \$10 million. Other threshold values for this variable were also investigated, but this did not change the results in a significant manner.

27

regulatory approval times in the United Kingdom and the United States such that

(3) $\qquad NDA_i^* = \beta_0 + \beta_1 NDA_i + u_{i2}$,
    with $0 < \beta_1 < 1$,

where

NDA_i^* = regulatory approval time for the ith NCE in the United Kingdom,

NDA_i = regulatory approval time for the ith NCE in the United States, and

u_{i2} = a random error term.

Then, by definition,

(4) $\qquad LA_i = NDA_i - NDA_i^*$.

Combining equations (3) and (4), one obtains

(5) $\qquad LA_i = -\beta_0 + (1 - \beta_1)NDA_i - u_{i2}$.

The final component of the U.S.-U.K. introduction lag, LF_i, encompasses any nonregulatory time delays in initiating required testing, filing applications, and so on in the United States versus the United Kingdom. It is not completely clear how these lags vary systematically with specific firm or product characteristics. Accordingly, one working hypothesis would be that they vary in a random manner across our cross-sectional sample of new drug entities. There does appear to be some propensity, however, for firms to market new drug entities in their home or a neighboring market first. Hence there may be some *nonregulatory* introduction lag for the United States on this account in the case of foreign drugs, but at the same time, the greater the potential economic gains from a new drug, the greater the incentives for firms to avoid nonregulatory (and regulatory) lags in large markets like the United States. This would suggest the following structure for LF_i:

(6) $\qquad LF_i = \gamma_0 + \gamma_1 FOR_i + \gamma_2 MKT_i + u_{i3}$,
    with $\gamma_1 > 0$, $\gamma_2 < 0$,

where

u_{i3} = a random error term.

The hypothetical effects of these two variables on LF_i are similar in direction to their effects on LD_i discussed above, so they do not change the predicted relationship between the total lag and these factors.

In order to obtain the relation for the total introduction lag, we can now substitute equations (2a), (5) and (6) into equation (1). This yields

(7) $\quad LAG_i = b_0 + b_1FOR_i + b_2RANK_i + b_3MKT_i + b_4NDA_i + v_i$, with $b_1 > 0, b_2 < 0, b_3 < 0$, and $0 < b_4 < 1$.

This is the basic functional form that will be analyzed here.

In light of the dynamic shifts observed above in firm behavior during the post-1962 period (Tables 6–8), equation (7) was estimated separately for the two subperiods 1963–1967 and 1968–1973.[22] The estimated equation coefficients in the two periods turned out to be significantly different statistically, and the results of each period will be considered separately.

For the 1963–1967 period, the estimated coefficients are presented in the first row of Table 9. All of the variables take on the expected sign except for the *MKT* variable, which is positive but statistically insignificant. The performance of the *NDA* variable is of particular interest. The estimated coefficient on this variable, which is statistically significant at the 1 percent level, indicates that for each month increase in NDA approval in this country, there was a 0.67 month increase in the introduction lag with the United Kingdom. The mean lag in U.S.-U.K. NCE introductions for this period was nine months, while the average regulatory approval time in the United States was twenty-three months with a range of four months to eighty-seven. The importance of the *NDA* variable to the explanatory power is demonstrated by the large drop in the $\bar{R}^2$ statistic when this variable is omitted from the estimated equation (row 2 of Table 9).

Of the other variables in the first equation of Table 9, the dummy variable for foreign origin takes the expected positive sign and is also statistically significant. The estimated coefficient on this variable indicates that, all other things being equal, the additional lag on a foreign-discovered NCE over a U.S.-discovered one was approximately one-and-

---

[22] The year 1973 was selected as the terminal point for the second period for two reasons. First, it is the last year for which information on all the independent variables was available. Second, in order to minimize any truncation bias, it is desirable to have some additional years on introduction dates in the United Kingdom beyond the end point on U.S. introduction dates included in our sample. Otherwise, the final few years of the sample period would include those mutual NCE introductions already in the United Kingdom (*re* U.S. introduction *lags*), while at the same time excluding those U.S. introductions yet to be introduced in the United Kingdom (*re* U.S. introduction *leads*). Because U.K. introduction dates were available through 1976, and were used in calculating the lags here, any such truncation bias should be very minor.

TABLE 9

DETERMINANTS OF THE LAG IN NCE INTRODUCTIONS BETWEEN THE UNITED STATES AND THE UNITED KINGDOM

Period	Constant	FOR_i	$RANK_i$	MKT_i	NDA_i	$FNDA_i$	$\bar{R}^2$
1963–67	−11.4	20.0 (2.38)*	−16.3 (1.93)	10.5 (1.21)	0.67 (2.75)**	—	.21
1963–67	3.7	20.3 (2.36)*	−16.2 (1.87)	9.6 (1.08)	—	—	.11
1968–73	0.1	30.9 (3.45)**	−9.2 (0.91)	−20.3 (2.03)*	0.80 (3.20)*	—	.40
1968–73	11.1	12.6 (0.82)	−10.8 (1.06)	−18.0 (1.89)	0.27 (0.51)	0.78 (1.47)	.42
1968–73	16.9	7.0 (0.58)	−11.7 (1.17)	−18.0 (1.81)	—	1.05 (3.50)**	.43

NOTES: Estimation of the regression equation, $LAG_i = b_0 + b_1FOR_i + b_2RANK_i + b_3MKT_i + b_4NDA_i + v_i$, where variables in parentheses are t values; * = Statistically significant at 5 percent level (two-tailed test); ** = Statistically significant at 1 percent level (two-tailed test).

LAG_i = the lag (+ or −) in months between the time of introduction in the U.K. and U.S. of the ith NCE.
FOR_i = a dummy variable taking on the value 1 if the ith NCE is of foreign origin and 0 otherwise.
$RANK_i$ = a dummy variable taking on the value 1 if the FDA has ranked the ith NCE as an important therapeutic advance and 0 otherwise.
MKT_i = a dummy variable taking on the value 1 if the ith NCE achieved $10 million in sales during its first three years after introduction and 0 otherwise.
NDA_i = U.S. regulatory approval time (in months) for the ith NCE.
$FNDA_i$ = FOR_i times NDA_i.

a-half years. The estimated coefficient on drugs ranked as important therapeutic advances (the *RANK* variable) is negative in value, suggesting a shorter lag for such drugs. This coefficient (with t value equal to 1.93) borders on statistical significance using a two-tailed test and would be statistically significant with a one-tailed test.

The final variable in this estimated equation, *MKT*, takes a positive value (with t value equal to 1.21), which is contrary to a priori expectations. The 1963–1967 period was a transitional one, however, in which U.S. firms in particular turned gradually to first introducing their NCEs abroad. Thus, the positive coefficient for the MKT may reflect the fact that firms had stronger economic incentives to switch rapidly to foreign introduction of products with large potential markets here and abroad. This would explain the positive coefficient.

Several variants on equation (7) were estimated for this period, including a specification with foreign slope dummies on the *NDA* variable, but this was not statistically significant. Various other formulations of the *MKT* and *RANK* variables were also tried, but these did not change the results in a material way.

The third row of Table 9 presents the coefficient estimates on equation (7) for the 1968–1973 period. This equation exhibits qualitative properties similar to those of the equation for the earlier period. However, the *MKT* variable now takes on the expected negative sign and is statistically significant. The *FOR* and *NDA* variables continue to be positively associated with the introduction lag and are statistically significant. Finally, the *RANK* variable continues to have a negative sign, but now with a t value less than one.

One major difference observed for the 1968–1973 period, however, is that when a foreign slope dummy is added to the *NDA* variable it tends to dominate this variable's statistical significance. This is apparent from the equations presented in rows (4) and (5) of Table 9. These estimated coefficients indicate that the observed lag associated with the *NDA* variable is significant for foreign but not U.S. drugs in the 1968 to 1973 period.

The source of this observed difference in the significance of the *NDA* variable for U.S.- and foreign-discovered drugs is not obvious. In the case of U.S.-discovered drugs, the nonsignificance of this variable could reflect the fact that by the late 1960s, U.S. firms had learned enough about FDA requirements to reduce considerably the delays at the final approval stage relative to other countries. In other words, the primary effects of U.S. regulation by that time could have been shifted backward to earlier stages of the innovational process (as, for example, to the clinical development of these new NCEs).

But if this were the primary explanation for this finding, why would it not also hold for foreign-discovered and foreign-developed drugs as well? The situation for these drugs differed from the situation for U.S. drugs in at least one very important aspect. Throughout this period, the FDA did not accept any clinical trials done in foreign countries as evidence in support of a drug application. Hence, a drug of foreign origin, whether introduced into the United States by a subsidiary of a foreign parent firm or through a licensing arrangement with a U.S. firm, had to undergo significant duplicate clinical testing in this country before gaining regulatory approval. Faced with this situation, the sponsoring firm may have opted for filing its NDAs on the basis of minimal duplicative testing in the United States and then engaging in a negotiation process with the FDA on the amount of duplicate testing actually necessary to gain approval. The high coefficient value on *FNDA* in rows (4) and (5) of Table 9 could therefore be a proxy for this phenomenon.

Some evidence consistent with this latter hypothesis is provided by comparing the average elapsed time between the beginning of clinical trials in the United States (that is, the first filing of the IND application) and the filing of an NDA for U.S.- and foreign-discovered drugs. For the 1968 to 1973 period, this averaged thirty-three months for the foreign-discovered drugs and forty-four months for the U.S.-discovered drugs in our sample. At the same time, the regulatory approval time was longer for foreign-discovered drugs (twenty-five months against twenty months for U.S.-discovered drugs).[23] Finally, the variation in regulatory approval times was considerably greater for foreign-discovered than for U.S.-discovered drugs.

In any event, the regression analysis presented in Table 9, which is the first statistical analysis (to my knowledge) on the determinants of drug lag, presents a number of interesting results. First, the overall pattern is generally consistent with the hypothesis that regulation has had a significant impact on introduction lag in NCEs between the United States and the United Kingdom. Second, these results underscore the much greater lags experienced by foreign-discovered drugs in entering the U.S. market than for those discovered in the United States. Third, given the statistical insignificance of the *RANK* variable (especially in the second time period), there appears to be little difference in the lags associated with drugs ranked as significant therapeutic advances

---

[23] Because the IND process was initated only in 1964, no accurate information on total development time exists for the earlier period. The regulatory approval time in the earlier period was identical for foreign-discovered and U.S.-discovered drugs in our sample—twenty-three months.

compared with those seen as providing more modest gains. This question is analyzed in more detail in the section that follows.

These results also suggest a number of interesting directions for future research. These include an analysis of the way the lag in NCE introductions is influenced by different modes of technology transfer (parent-subsidiary as against licensing of marketing arrangements) and by the way the organization of multinationals explicitly affects the NCE introduction process. Some data are currently being collected with the objective of analyzing these issues.

The Drug Quality Issue. As we noted, FDA officials have argued that the drug lag has been associated primarily with drugs of modest or insignificant therapeutic importance and that its consequences for the health of U.S. patients are therefore minimal. Our regression analysis in the last section, however, failed to reveal a statistically significant relation supporting this assertion. In particular, drugs rated as important therapeutic gains by the FDA did not have significantly shorter lags than other NCEs in our sample.

To focus more directly on this issue, I have constructed in Table 10 the specific U.S.-U.K. lead and lag pattern for all those NCEs ranked by the FDA as important therapeutic advances. The table has the same general format as Tables 6 through 8. The United Kingdom seems the most appropriate country to select for this analysis because it has regulatory standards most comparable in quality to those of the FDA.

The data show a pattern qualitatively similar to that observed in Table 6 which includes all mutual NCE introductions for the two countries. During the first period, more NCEs ranked as important therapeutic gains were introduced in the United States before they were introduced in the United Kingdom rather than the other way around. This is a similar finding to the results on all NCEs previously observed for this period, given that the vast majority of these important drugs were of U.S. origin (17 of 24).

What is particularly striking about Table 10, however, is the dramatic shift occurring in the introduction pattern in the second period. In this period, ten of the seventeen NCEs rated as important gains by the FDA were introduced first in the United Kingdom, three were introduced here and abroad in the same year, and only three were first introduced in the United States. The propensity for first introduction of significant NCEs abroad is thus much greater than that for the overall sample of NCEs in this latter period.

Considerable insight into the reason for this observed pattern is provided by examining the source of seventeen NCEs ranked as im-

TABLE 10

COMPARISON OF NCE INTRODUCTION DATES, UNITED STATES
AND UNITED KINGDOM, FOR DRUGS RANKED BY THE FDA
AS IMPORTANT THERAPEUTIC GAINS, 1963–1973

		Number (Percent) of Common NCEs Introduced in United Kingdom			
Period	Total	Before United States	Same year	After United States	*Not Introduced in the United Kingdom*
1963–1967	22 (100)	7 (32)	5 (23)	10 (45)	2
1968–1973	16 (100)	10 (63)	3 (19)	3 (19)	1

NOTE: Three entities classified as important gains by FDA (Softconbandage lens in 1973, Methylmetharcrylate in 1971, and mafenide acetate in 1970) were omitted from our sample because these entities are not considered NCEs by deHaen or Wardell. New salts or esters of previously marketed products are omitted.

SOURCE: Information on NCE introductions in the United States and United Kingdom were obtained from data compiled by Paul deHaen, Inc., and from data supplied by Professor William Wardell (obtained through questionnaire surveys). FDA classification of NCEs as important therapeutic gains taken from appendix to FDA Commissioner Schmidt, "Testimony before U.S. Senate Subcommittee on Health" (*Kennedy Hearings*), August 16, 1974.

portant gains during this period. Of the seventeen drugs, 7.5 were U.S. discovered, 7.5 were foreign discovered, one was a duplicate discovery, and two were known drugs. Moreover, all of the foreign-discovered drugs ranked as important gains were introduced into the United Kingdom at least three years or more before they became available here. The increased importance of foreign countries as sources of drugs representing major gains, then, is the main factor accounting for this dramatic shift in the 1968–1973 period. There also was an increased propensity in the second period for U.S.-discovered NCEs to have their first introduction abroad, but this factor was not so important as the other in producing the dramatic shift shown in Table 10.[24]

Of course, one cannot attribute the consistently long introduction lags in foreign-discovered drugs solely to regulatory factors; clearly they result in part from industrial choice and strategy. But it is important to note that significant NCEs discovered and developed in the United Kingdom, Switzerland, and Italy took three to six years longer to get into this country than into the United Kingdom. Many of these NCEs originated in countries now having relatively high regulatory standards (such as the United Kingdom). Hence, one might have expected a relatively speedy regulatory process in the United States but this was apparently not the case.

The balancing of regulatory benefits against costs is of course beyond the scope of the present inquiry. To the extent that these long lags in important drugs were caused in part by the requirement that firms carry out duplicate testing in the United States, they would appear to be an excessive and unwarranted cost of regulation.

During the last two years the FDA has announced its intention of pursuing a more liberal policy toward the acceptance of foreign trials. It remains to be seen what the exact effect of this shift in policy will be. In light of the results observed in Table 10, it would appear to be a significant reform for expediting the availability of important new therapies to U.S. patients.

Summary and Conclusions

Several interesting findings emerge from our analysis. First, the data on introduction dates of NCEs here and in Europe clearly show that the United States has shifted from leading to lagging the United Kingdom

---

[24] Of the 7.5 U.S.-discovered drugs ranked as significant therapeutic gains in the second period, 3 were introduced first in the United States, 2.5 were introduced first in the United Kingdom, and 2 were introduced in both countries in the same year.

and Germany in the post-1962 period. The United States still generally leads France in the case of U.S.-discovered NCE introductions, but not in foreign-discovered ones. Second, the analysis further indicates that the lag with Europe is not confined to drugs with little or modest medical gain but also includes drugs the FDA itself ranks as significant therapeutic advances. Third, there is evidence, both from regression analysis and indirectly from the changing pattern exhibited by U.S.-discovered NCEs, that regulation has been a major factor contributing to this lag. Finally, the analysis indicates that regulation has had an especially strong impact on the introduction lag for foreign-discovered drugs over this period.

This last finding is especially significant because foreign-discovered NCEs accounted for one-half of the drugs rated therapeutically significant by the FDA during the most recent period analyzed (1968–1973). These medically significant drugs of foreign origin were all introduced into the United States with very long lags—three to six years after they were introduced into the United Kingdom. However, one main regulatory obstacle to the introduction of foreign drugs that was operating during this period—the FDA's policy of not accepting foreign clinical trials—has apparently been liberalized somewhat in the last few years.

These results suggest a number of possible directions for further research. It would be desirable, for example, to develop some additional measures of regulatory stringency, not only for the United States, but also for foreign countries. There is some indication from the literature that regulation in Europe is moving closer in character to regulation in the United States, and this would be worth examining in a formal way. It would also be interesting to consider more formally how the structural characteristics of multinational organizations and different modes of technology transfer affect the rate of diffusion across countries. Finally, it would be quite instructive to perform an analysis similar to that undertaken above for several other countries—especially Japan, which now has the second largest market in pharmaceuticals but very different regulatory and institutional characteristics from those of the European countries studied here.

Government Policy and the Transfer of Pharmaceutical Technology among Developed Countries

Josef C. Brada

This paper presents some evidence on the way the flow of pharmaceutical technology among developed Western countries is influenced by the foreign and domestic policies of developed and developing nations. The evidence is based on a series of extensive interviews with the executives of ten large pharmaceutical firms—two U.S. affiliates of foreign firms and eight U.S. multinationals. Thus, the material presented represents the views of pharmaceutical industry executives on the way government policies influence the conduct of their companies' foreign operations. No effort was made to elicit evaluations of these policies nor was the study presented as having direct policy implications. The author bears all responsibility for synthesis of the interviews and for the conclusions drawn from this synthesis.[1]

The International Operations of Pharmaceutical Firms

Organization. Most of the firms interviewed are also engaged in business activities other than the production and distribution of ethical drugs. Many of these activities—such as producing animal health products, animal feed supplements, proprietary drugs, and chemicals—are natural extensions of the production of ethical drugs. Some firms, however, have moved farther afield into cosmetics, food products, and nonchemical manufacturing. In either case, most of the firms are organized by product division, and for all of them the pharmaceutical division is the

[1] The research underlying this paper was carried out under a consultantship to the Organization for Economic Cooperation and Development. I am indebted to John Dunning for guidance in formulating the study and to my sometime colleague, Robert G. Hawkins, for assistance in its implementation. The New York University Project on the Multinational Corporation in the World Economy provided financial support for the interviews on which this paper is based.

The most valuable assistance I received in pursuing this research was provided by those pharmaceutical executives who consented to participate in the interviews. Since one of the ground rules for the interviews was anonymity for the participants, my thanks must be less personal though no less sincere than usual.

largest in sales and profits. These pharmaceutical divisions (or in cases where there are no other products, the whole company) are divided on a regional basis—usually in three to six regions spanning the globe. In some companies, the regional organizations are divisions of the company and report directly to top management. In others, an international division serves as an intermediary between top management and the regional organizations. In addition to their foreign divisions, all U.S. multinational pharmaceutical companies have domestic divisions. Many also maintain separate divisions for research and development; those that do not generally conduct research and development within their domestic divisions.

All U.S. firms interviewed maintain the bulk of their foreign-operation staff functions at corporate headquarters, while line personnel are located abroad. Significant differences exist among companies in the number of staff and technical personnel located abroad; as might be expected, the greater the volume and complexity of foreign operations, the greater the number. All companies maintain regional management centers overseas, housing staff and line personnel and often technical staff as well. Some companies finance the activities of these centers from central funds, while others require regional affiliates to contribute some or all of the funds required.

All companies maintain strong central control over research and development activities and over quality control. The financial performance of affiliates is subject to frequent evaluations under uniform reporting procedures established by the parent firm (though these uniform procedures do not necessarily ensure interaffiliate comparability).

Foreign Involvement. Foreign activity plays a significant role in the business of all the companies interviewed. Although individual firms do not as a rule disclose the volume of pharmaceutical sales and profits their foreign operations generate, it can be inferred from available information that foreign operations for the ten firms in question account for 30 to 50 percent of sales and profits. Since corporate data are not available, we must rely on industry data here. Table 1 shows the domestic and foreign sales of the member firms of the Pharmaceutical Manufacturers Association. The ratio of foreign sales to total sales has risen steadily for the industry during the 1970s, even though including the U.S. sales of foreign-firm affiliates in with domestic sales imparts a downward bias to the ratio.[2]

---

[2] Harold A. Clymer, "The Economic and Regulatory Climate: U.S. and Overseas Trends," in Robert Helms, ed., *Drug Development and Marketing* (Washington:

TABLE 1

HUMAN-USE ETHICAL PHARMACEUTICAL SALES AND RESEARCH AND
DEVELOPMENT EXPENDITURES FOR HUMAN AND VETERINARY
PRODUCTS, PHARMACEUTICAL MANUFACTURERS ASSOCIATION MEMBER
FIRMS, 1961–1976

| | *Pharmaceutical Sales (millions of current dollars)* | | | | *Foreign Dosage Sales as a Percent of Total* | *Global R&D Expenditures (millions of current dollars)* |
| | Domestic | | Foreign | | | |
Year	Dosage	Bulk	Dosage	Bulk		
1961	1954	127	627	63	25	238
1962	2199	113	640	65	23	251
1963	2317	122	731	58	24	282
1964	2479	125	806	64	25	298
1965	2779	161	930	69	25	351
1966	3011	167	1077	85	27	402
1967	3226	167	1279	72	28	448
1968	3655	153	1417	77	28	485
1969	4008	127	1618	84	29	549
1970	4322	122	1890	91	31	619
1971	4667	129	2113	110	32	684
1972	5018	118	2379	125	33	726
1973	5507	137	2951	127	35	825
1974	6083	190	3474	209	37	942
1975	6895	193	4245	214	39	1062
1976	7669	198	4686	222	38	1164

SOURCES: Pharmaceutical Manufacturers Association, *Prescription Drug Industry Factbook* (Washington: Pharmaceutical Manufacturers Association, various years); Pharmaceutical Manufacturers Association, *Annual Survey Report* (Washington: Pharmaceutical Manufacturers Association, various years).

None of the firms interviewed makes significant imports or exports of pharmaceuticals in dosage form into or out of the United States—indeed all firms indicated that such activity was being discontinued, and for several it has already ceased. Similarly, imports and exports of bulk pharmaceuticals or active ingredients are of minor importance and, where they occur, often result from temporary shortages or from the availability of excess productive capacity in the United States or abroad.

American Enterprise Institute, 1975), p. 143. Clymer estimates that the exclusion of the sales of U.S. affiliates of foreign firms would have raised the percentage of sales for American firms from 33 percent to 38 percent in 1972.

Some exceptions exist for plants that have specialized production facilities for particular drugs, but such instances are rare. The most important export activity of U.S. pharmaceutical firms is the sale of chemicals to foreign affiliates, which then convert the chemicals into active pharmaceutical agents. There are several reasons for this pattern of trade.

Tariff and nontariff barriers. The firms responding to our interviews reported that in many countries tariffs on dosage forms are prohibitive and that the nontariff barriers against the importation of dosage pharmaceuticals are extensive. Tariffs on bulk pharmaceuticals tend to be lower than those levied on dosage forms, and the stringency of nontariff barriers is also somewhat less for bulk. Tariffs on chemicals are lower yet, and the nontariff barriers imposed by drug laws also lose much of their importance.

Drug laws. U.S. drug laws prohibit the exportation of dosage form and bulk pharmaceuticals unless the drug has been approved for use in the United States; that is, a U.S. pharmaceutical manufacturer that obtains approval for a new drug abroad but not in the United States cannot export the drug from the United States. Consequently, if the company is to sell the drug abroad, it must produce it at one of its bulk plants outside the United States. An attractive alternative is to ship the active ingredient out of the United States in the form of a chemical intermediate, which is then turned into the bulk pharmaceutical abroad. The feasibility of such a procedure depends on the process used in producing the pharmaceutical, because in some processes it is not possible to interrupt the chemical reaction.

In view of the economic and legal obstacles in the United States to exporting drugs to developed-country markets, all respondents make extensive use of the productive capabilities of wholly-owned affiliates located in these countries. Most of the firms interviewed have some foreign operations other than wholly-owned affiliates—joint ventures or partnerships for sales and distribution and licensing—although such operations are undertaken with some reluctance. The wholly-owned affiliates are viewed as best suited to protecting the firm's products, reputation, and economic interests.

Foreign Affiliates of Pharmaceutical Firms. Although our respondents did not provide detailed financial information on their foreign affiliates in developed countries, industry data reveal that such affiliates tend to be large relative to the affiliates these firms operate in less developed countries. According to the Pharmaceutical Manufacturers Association,

29 percent of U.S. firms' affiliates were located in western Europe and 5 percent in Canada. The European affiliates accounted for some 55 percent of those firms' foreign assets and the Canadian affiliates for 12 percent.[3]

There are three main forms of productive activities that American pharmaceutical firms locate abroad: bulk plants, dosage and bottling plants, and sales and promotional activities.

Bulk plants. Bulk plants are the largest and technologically most sophisticated units in the pharmaceutical production process. They produce the active ingredients for the company's drug products. These plants must be designed for maximum flexibility because they must produce a wide variety of chemicals in quantities varying from several pounds to a ton or more a year and they must be adaptable for the production of drugs the company may develop in the future.

All respondents have one or more bulk plants in the United States and one (or, less frequently, several) located in developed western countries. Countries where bulk plants are located include Belgium, France, Ireland, Italy, Japan, Spain, and the United Kingdom. Ireland is an attractive site because of tax and investment incentives and the tariff advantages for Irish exports to the European Community.

Although bulk plants located abroad are, on average, smaller than the firms' bulk plants in the United States, they are as technically advanced and in nearly all instances could produce the drugs made in U.S. plants. The general business operations of the bulk plants abroad differ from operations in the United States in two ways. First, in a number of cases, the foreign-based bulk plants sell bulk pharmaceuticals to users other than company dosage plants; such sales are quite rare in the United States. Second, bulk plants located abroad export a much greater proportion of their output than do their U.S. counterparts. Thus, for example, bulk plants located in countries like Ireland, where the domestic market is small, are designed to provide bulk pharmaceuticals to company affiliates in all of western Europe, Africa, and even the Middle East.

Most U.S. respondents believe that the centralized production of bulk pharmaceuticals promotes significant economies of scale and flexibility. As one respondent put it, given no tariffs, nontariff barriers, or government regulations, his company would find it most advantageous

---

[3] Calculated from Pharmaceutical Manufacturers Association, *Pharmaceutical Manufacturers Association Factbook, 1973* (Washington: Pharmaceutical Manufacturers Association, 1974) and from *U.S. Direct Investment Abroad, 1966: Final Data* (Washington: U. S. Department of Commerce, 1968).

to produce all its bulk pharmaceuticals in one or several nearby and closely coordinated bulk plants in the United States.

Dosage plants. Dosage plants use the active ingredients produced by the bulk plants to formulate capsules, pills, suppositories, and so on. Dosage plants require smaller capital investment than bulk plants, and their technology appears to be more readily transferable abroad. Nevertheless, a dosage plant does embody extremely sophisticated techniques of quality control, formulation, and adaptation of drugs to local needs, medical practice, and climatic conditions. All respondents have several dosage plants in developed countries, the number ranging from six to twelve. Respondents maintain more dosage plants than bulk plants abroad because of the greater restrictions and higher tariffs that most developed countries have imposed on imports of dosage pharmaceuticals and because, for obvious reasons, dosage plants do not enjoy the increasing economies of scale that bulk plants do.

There seem to be few differences between the technical capabilities of dosage plants located in the United States and those located abroad. What minor differences there are suggest no appreciable advantage in capability between domestic and overseas plants, although overseas plants do have one capability not required by plants in the United States—the ability to convert certain types of imported chemicals into bulk-form pharmaceuticals.

The U.S. plants and those located abroad both produce the full line of drugs for the markets they serve. Among the dosage plants, there is little effort at specialization and exchange. Those abroad generally export large portions of their production, while those located in the United States do not. Dosage plants located in developed countries export not only to other developed countries but also to less developed countries. In the latter case, there appears to be a certain amount of geographic specialization, with plants in the United Kingdom and France exporting to those countries' former colonies, and plants in Italy serving the Mediterranean basin.

Other facilities. Respondent firms also maintain less sophisticated installations abroad such as bottling and packaging plants as well as sales establishments for the company's products. The bulk of the activities not carried out through wholly-owned subsidiaries fall in these categories.

Research and Development. The costs of discovering new drugs and developing them into marketable products are tremendously high. As a result, U.S. pharmaceutical firms devote a higher percentage of their sales dollar to research and development than firms in any other

TABLE 2

RESEARCH AND DEVELOPMENT EXPENDITURES, PMA MEMBER FIRMS
(millions of current dollars)

	1968	1971	1973	1976
Company-financed R&D expenditures for human-use pharmaceuticals:				
Amount spent in United States	410.4	576.5	643.8	902.9
Within firm	353.8	510.1	565.8	794.6
Outside firm	46.6	66.4	77.0	108.3
Amount spent abroad	39.1	52.3	108.7	164.9
Within firm	31.8	45.8	92.1	145.1
Outside firm	7.3	6.5	16.6	19.8
Total human-use R&D	449.5	628.8	752.5	1,067.8
Company-financed R&D expenditures for veterinary-use pharmaceuticals:				
Amount spent in United States	32.3	43.1	53.7	71.4
Within firm	30.8	40.1	50.6	65.0
Outside firm	1.5	3.0	3.1	6.4
Amount spent abroad	3.3	4.8	8.2	15.4
Within firm	3.1	4.6	7.9	14.6
Outside firm	0.2	0.2	0.3	0.8
Total veterinary R&D	35.7	47.9	61.9	86.8
U.S. government contracts for company-conducted R&D				
	9.6	7.1	10.6	9.1
Total corporate R&D	494.8	683.8	825.0	1,163.7

SOURCE: Pharmaceutical Manufacturers Association, *Annual Survey Report* (Washington: Pharmaceutical Manufacturers Association, various years).

industry but computers.[4] Moreover, as may be seen from Table 2, nearly all pharmaceutical research is financed by the firms themselves: little if any is undertaken on behalf of the government or with its financial support.

Over the past two decades, the cost of discovering new drugs has risen steadily. To the extent that it is the government rather than the state of scientific knowledge that has raised the costs of drug discovery and development, it is to be expected that U.S. firms might react by

---

[4] "R&D Spending Patterns," *Business Week*, July 3, 1978.

TABLE 3
AVERAGE RESEARCH AND DEVELOPMENT EXPENDITURES AND SALES BY FIRM SIZE, SAMPLE OF PMA FIRMS, 1973 AND 1976

Size of R&D budget	Domestic			Foreign			Total		
	Average R&D expenditures	Average sales	R&D sales ratio	Average R&D expenditures	Average sales	R&D sales ratio	Average R&D expenditures	Average sales	R&D sales ratio
	(millions of current dollars)			(millions of current dollars)			(millions of current dollars)		
1973									
More than $20 million	35.6	272.7	.130	5.7	191.5	.030	41.3	464.2	.089
$10–$20 million	14.6	109.3	.134	2.2	54.4	.040	16.8	163.7	.103
$ 5–$10 million	6.8	65.6	.107	0.6	16.8	.036	7.4	82.3	.090
$ 1–$ 5 million	2.4	34.3	.070	0.0	2.4	.000	2.4	36.7	.067
Less than $1 million	0.4	16.2	.024	0.0	0.4	.000	0.4	20.4	.020
Firm average	14.5	118.3	.122	2.1	16.6	.031	16.6	186.9	.089
1976									
More than $30 million	46.9	360.2	.130	9.9	295.6	.033	56.8	655.8	.087
$10–$30 million	15.9	107.3	.148	2.5	30.3	.083	18.4	137.6	.134
$ 1–$10 million	4.4	47.2	.093	0.2	11.4	.018	4.6	58.6	.078
Less than $1 million	0.3	12.9	.023	0.0	5.8	.000	0.3	18.7	.016
Firm average	21.6	167.2	.129	4.0	114.4	.035	25.6	281.6	.091

SOURCE: Pharmaceutical Manufacturers Association, *Annual Survey Report* (Washington: Pharmaceutical Manufacturers Association, various years).

moving research and development activities abroad so as to take advantage of a more favorable regulatory climate there. Table 3 gives some industry evidence on the amount of research done in the United States and abroad. The firms interviewed in this study all have research and development budgets in excess of $5 million, and all make some R&D expenditures abroad.

New product discovery. All respondents have more than one corporate research laboratory, the number varying from two to six. The firms actually maintain only one or two major research laboratories; the remainder are small specialized laboratories conducting research on specific diseases best studied on site. The home laboratory of the U.S. firms is larger than their labs abroad, but the U.S. affiliates of foreign firms have research laboratories comparable in size to those of the parent firm. Despite determined efforts to maintain strict central direction over research activities, no company reported having any conscious policy of developing specialization in a particular area of research at a given laboratory, although such specialization could occur because of the process by which innovation takes place or because of host-country needs.

Although the management of research is quite similar for all firms interviewed, financing and ownership policies for research facilities vary considerably. Some firms maintain central ownership of foreign research facilities and finance the activities of these facilities out of central funds. Other firms vest ownership rights of foreign laboratories in the local affiliate and require that the affiliate finance the laboratory, but it is common for the parent company to provide funds for major expansion of research activities. Because of French laws prohibiting the payment of royalties for research done by foreign parents of affiliates in France, firms that maintain central ownership of research facilities elsewhere have opted to have their French subsidiaries support their own research facilities.

Preclinical and clinical research. Preclinical and clinical research are generally carried out extramurally under contract with individual researchers. These contracts usually are centrally funded and controlled. U.S. firms reported they are increasing the amount of clinical research undertaken abroad for a number of reasons. Costs of clinical research tend to be lower abroad than in this country, and some respondents indicated that foreign researchers are more willing to undertake such research than their U.S. counterparts. Moreover, government approval for the required test often may be obtained more easily or more rapidly elsewhere than in the United States. Carrying out clinical tests abroad also helps a company penetrate foreign markets. A number of respondents also pointed out that by carrying out clinical tests abroad, they demonstrate the company's commitment to doing business in a genuinely multinational way and to the progress of medical science in less developed countries.

Formulation research. Research on developing and improving the dosage forms of a drug and adapting them to local needs (formulation research) is carried out in three types of facilities. Each U.S. firm interviewed has a central group for formulation research, located in the United States and financed out of central funds. A number of respondents also have a similar—though smaller—group located at one or several foreign affiliates. Still other respondents supplement the central group with regional research centers corresponding to the regional structure of the firm, with each regional center financed by the affiliates it serves. In this case, one of the primary functions of the regional centers is to assist the affiliates in developing dosage forms appropriate to their markets. Dosage plants themselves do much of their own formulation research, funded by the individual affiliate firm. Although formulation research is somewhat more decentralized geographically than new-product research, all new formulations (or changes in old formulations) must be submitted to the parent firm for approval, partly to guard against undesirable changes in formulation and partly to enable the parent firm to disseminate to all of its dosage plants the formulation improvements any one affiliate develops.

U.S. affiliates of foreign firms have formulation research capabilities similar to those of the parent firm, although their research is devoted almost exclusively to meeting the needs of the U.S. market. As in all other areas of research and development (save new-product discovery), it is the European parent rather than the U.S. affiliate that meets the needs of the firm's affiliates elsewhere.

Process development and improvement. The development and design of new processes for the production of drugs are organized in much the same way as formulation research. A central group, in some cases supplemented by regional groups, is charged with the design of new bulk and dosage plants. Moreover, although pharmaceutical firms rely on manufacturers of chemical processing equipment to supply standard needs, they do have the capacity to design unique process units when they are required. Both bulk plants and dosage plants have staff engineers to help design new plants and processes to improve old ones, and to integrate new processes into the existing plant.

Quality control. Quality control is the most centralized function in all firms interviewed. Standards are established centrally, and affiliates must then develop acceptable ways of meeting them.

Research Strategies. Most respondents indicated that one laboratory is sufficient for new product research. Several disagreed, however. Two large firms felt that at some point a research facility could become too large to manage effectively, and they had two research laboratories. A smaller firm indicated that it did not accept the economies-of-scale argument and that its perception of itself as an international firm led it to do research both in the United States and abroad.

The respondents cited three advantages in having laboratories abroad: such laboratories serve as listening posts for scientific trends and developments abroad, they enable the company to make use of a wider variety of scientific approaches, and they give the company access to the excellence of the scientific community in the foreign country. Despite these advantages, all firms expressed a strong reluctance to establish new research facilities abroad. One reason given is that few countries have sufficiently developed scientific support to meet the needs of a large-scale facility. The problem is further complicated by the fact that it is desirable to locate laboratories near bulk plants. Finally, some respondents questioned whether a new laboratory could be expected to make any significant breakthroughs in its first eight to ten years of operation—which argues, of course, against establishing new labs at all.

As a result, U.S. firms have foreign research laboratories primarily where they have acquired a foreign pharmaceutical firm with a research laboratory. Even when the parent firm believes that economies of scale do exist in pharmaceutical research, respondents have maintained (and in some cases made significant expenditures to expand) foreign laboratories obtained through corporate acquisition. The U.S. affiliates of foreign firms differed significantly from this pattern in that the research laboratories in the United States were not obtained through corporate mergers or acquisition but were established within the affiliate by the parent firm. Reasons given were the need to tap the potential of the U.S. scientific community and the fact that the size of the U.S. market made it financially feasible to establish and support a large research facility here.

All firms interviewed, as we would expect, place great emphasis on research, though it may be noted that for some companies the canons of prudent management involve diversification into nonpharmaceutical activities. No respondent gave a very clear explanation of how it determines the amount of resources it expends on pharmaceutical research. But it is clear that determining factors include the past pattern of such expenditures, current profits, industry trends in research and development, the competitiveness of the firm's drugs, and the corporate philosophy toward research and development. One firm (a successful one) indicated that research and development funds tend to be a residual, determined after other needs are met. This does not imply that the firm views research as unimportant; it means that all surplus funds are added to the already budgeted expenditures for research.

Although all respondents reported that the costs of discovering and developing new drugs had risen (thus forcing reductions in the number of research projects undertaken), there was disagreement about the causes of increased costs and their consequences for pharmaceutical research. Some respondents felt that the major force increasing the costs of drug development is the increased stringency of government drug registration regulation. Other firms contended that government regulations merely embody standards that the firms themselves would institute as a matter of good scientific practice. In this view, the cost increases are primarily the result of advances in pharmaceutical and medical practice—though government regulations that delay tests or require excessive or unnecessary tests also play a role.

Some firms stated that the decline in the number of projects might reduce the return to research and development expenditures sufficiently to decrease the firm's commitment to pharmaceutical research. Others felt that the reduction in the number of projects would be offset by the fact that new drugs would be more profitable than drugs developed ten to fifteen years ago. These firms believe the drugs currently under development are better, will have fewer competitors on the market, and will enjoy longer market lives than drugs developed in the past. Advances in science have changed the discovery process from one of trial and error experiments with compounds in order to see whether they have therapeutic properties to one where compounds possibly having therapeutic properties can be deduced by studying the properties of the disease. In addition, fewer projects are undertaken in order to discover so-called "me too" drugs, which replicate the therapeutic properties of drugs already on the market; instead, research is focused on discovering drugs that treat diseases for which no drugs as yet exist and drugs for which there is a large potential market.

Respondents also differ in the criteria they emphasize in selecting research projects. Some stress the worldwide market potential for drugs in certain therapeutic categories and the probability of success in discovering new drugs in those categories. Others place primary emphasis on therapeutic areas in which the firm has already established research expertise. Expansion of research activities into new therapeutic areas occurs less frequently in these firms than in those that allocate research funds on the basis of market potential for drugs in various categories. Finally, one firm reported that it attempts to maintain a viable research program in every therapeutic category and gives its research workers the freedom to undertake those projects they consider to be the most likely to yield significant results.

The International Transfer of Technology

All respondents seek rapid diffusion of corporate technology to those affiliates that can make profitable use of it. The means of transfer vary according to the technology and (to a lesser degree) the firm involved.

New Products. Affiliate managers are kept informed of the status of new drugs being developed by the parent firm by means of circulars, regional meetings, and other ordinary techniques. The parent firm also provides the basic information required by affiliates to register and market the drug. In most firms, affiliate managers are free to decide whether they wish to undertake the production of a new drug for their market; managers may choose not to produce imitative drugs or drugs with a limited national market. The parent company may use moral suasion to induce affiliates to adopt a product that is required to carry out a global marketing strategy or to achieve economies of scale. One company differed from the "laissez-faire" policy in introducing new products abroad, preferring to have the corporate headquarters choose the first country of introduction on the basis of large market size, incidence of the disease the new drug treats, and, most important, the likelihood of a speedy approval of the drug by regulatory authorities in the country of introduction.

Process and Product Technology. Developments in process and product technology are disseminated through manuals prepared by the parent firm and through exchanges and meetings of experts. Any successful innovation affiliates develop must be submitted to the parent firm for approval. If the approval is granted, the innovation is incorporated into a manual pertaining to the manufacture of the product and disseminated to all other affiliates.

All respondents make concerted efforts to disseminate technology through exchanges of specialists, including engineering and technical specialists and also accountants, finance specialists, plant managers, production specialists, quality control people, and engineers from the various affiliates. In some companies, such meetings are held on a regular basis, in others less so; large companies tend to be more systematic in holding meetings. Product mix also has an influence on the frequency of exchanges. Companies that make extensive use of fermentation technology (which is a *biological* process) tend to place greater emphasis on meetings of experts from various bulk plants than do firms whose products are manufactured by chemical synthesis. The reason lies in the fact that plant operation has an important impact on yields from fermentation, while yields from synthesis reactions are relatively difficult to alter.

Interfirm Transfer of Technology. Transfers of product technology between firms takes place mainly through the exchange of licenses. All respondents reported that they had undertaken "swaps" of this sort, although their frequency differs greatly. All respondents have a marked preference for license swaps over simple sales of licenses, because they see significant benefits in acquiring new products through swaps—especially new products that will fill a gap in the firm's offerings in a given therapeutic category. These firms believe they have a marketing advantage if they are able to offer a range of products in a therapeutic category rather than only one or two. Firms also use swaps to supplement their own research efforts in a particular area or to help develop expertise in a new area. Several respondents indicated that their firms believe they could do a better job of marketing drugs than was done by the firms from which the drugs were acquired. In some cases, the swapping of licenses need not be immediate—indeed, a firm may remain in a debtor position for several years until it develops a drug the creditor firm wishes to acquire. Note that license swaps also involve royalties, which may be lump-sum payments for low-volume drugs or payments based on sales volume for high-volume products.

U.S. firms generally will seek to obtain worldwide rights to drugs they acquire from other firms. One respondent reported that the firm's expansion into world markets had been hampered by the fact that a large proportion of its U.S. product line had been obtained under limited license from foreign firms and could not be sold abroad. Consequently, the most desirable swap partners for U.S. firms are foreign firms with weak international sales networks. Several respondents indicated that as an alternative to a license exchange with such a firm, they might accept a joint venture for the worldwide sale of the foreign firm's drug through the U.S. firm's sales network. One respondent has a different approach to licensing: it mainly sells licenses to producers in markets it cannot serve through an affiliate or through exports. Exchanges of technology also take place through sales or exchanges of process technology or, very rarely, through joint research.

Patents and Royalties. All companies try to provide patent protection for new products early in the development stage. Although one company claimed to seek patent protection in every country where it could be obtained, most weighed the costs and benefits of obtaining patents in various countries on a product-by-product basis. The extent of protection for a given drug will depend on its therapeutic importance and the range of its potential market. Most firms expressed moderate satisfaction with the degree of patent protection in all the developed countries, with the exceptions of the lack of process protection in the United States and of product protection in Germany, and the lack of any protection in Italy.[5] Respondents with operations in Italy reported that they did not infringe on patents held by other firms and that only Italian firms infringed on their patents. All firms noted that the growing length of time between the discovery of a drug's therapeutic potential and its approval for marketing reduces the usefulness of patents for protecting the firm's technology because the drug would not be on the market for most of the length of the patent.

Generally, a parent company acquires worldwide rights for its products and then grants rights within a country to its affiliates. If an affiliate rather than the parent firm has discovered a new drug, several procedures are used. Some parents maintain cross-licensing agreements with their affiliates that have laboratories; in this case, the foreign affiliate that develops the drug would grant licenses to other foreign affiliates. Other parents purchase the rights to the new product from the affiliate, and the affiliate shares in the royalties paid by other affiliates in proportion to its contribution to the costs of bringing the drug to the market. Various national restrictions on royalty payments, however, have thrown this system into such disarray that several respondents expect the eventual demise of royalty payments.

Conclusions

The transfer of pharmaceutical technology between the United States and other developed countries takes place mainly through the establish-

---

[5] At the time of the interviews, patent protection for drugs was not available in Italy. In 1977, the Italian supreme court ruled that this prohibition against the patenting of drugs is unconstitutional.

ment and operation of production and research facilities in the other countries. In this respect, the pharmaceutical industry differs from industries in which exports are the initial means for exploiting corporate technology in foreign markets.

The movement of bulk plants out of the United States to other developed countries is influenced by tariffs (which are relatively unimportant) and by the regulatory policies of both the United States and the host countries.

Of greatest significance in the decision to locate bulk plants abroad are the regulatory climate in the United States and the prohibition against exporting unregistered drugs. If drugs could be approved more speedily in the United States, the export of bulk pharmaceuticals from the United States would be a viable alternative to the location of production facilities abroad. Or if U.S. regulations were changed to permit the export of any pharmaceutical to a country where its use is permitted by local authorities, it is likely that some of the drugs manufactured by bulk plants located abroad might be manufactured in the United States. It is instructive in this regard to observe the difference between the operation of U.S. and European pharmaceutical firms. Among the U.S. firms, the parent affiliates produce both for their own and for third-country markets. In contrast, the affiliates of European multinational companies located in the United States do no importing and exporting: the parent firm supplies bulk and dosage to its non-U.S. foreign affiliates. This pattern does not appear to result from production capacity or technical skill differences between affiliates of U.S. and European firms. If anything, the U.S. affiliates of European drug firms are larger and carry on more research than the European affiliates of U.S. firms. Thus, the pattern of exports does not result from any differences in the capabilities of U.S. and European affiliates but rather from differences in U.S. and European policies on drug exports.

The movement of dosage plants overseas seems to be influenced both by policy (mainly that of the host countries) and by economics. Tariff and nontariff barriers are important factors leading to the location of dosage plants both in developed and in developing countries, and decentralization of dosage production is consistent with the economic forces that influence the costs and benefits of particular patterns of production. It is likely that lowering trade barriers would lead to a small reduction in the number of dosage plants located abroad but not to large increases in exports of drugs from or imports of drugs into the United States.

There appears to be intense pressure on pharmaceutical firms to locate research facilities abroad both in developed and developing countries. This pressure, insofar as it relates to research laboratories, is resented by most firms for two reasons—first, because it generally takes a form (such as limitations on royalty payments by affiliates) that hinders the firm in obtaining fair compensation for its research and development investments; and second, because most firms view the establishment and operation of research laboratories abroad as expensive, difficult to coordinate, and (at least in the short run) unproductive.

The large foreign laboratories of U.S. firms were obtained through corporate acquisition, but there are few attractive foreign pharmaceutical acquisitions left for U.S. firms. Thus, the number of large research laboratories operated by U.S. firms abroad is unlikely to increase further. The pattern exhibited by European multinationals (in establishing major research facilities in the United States) will probably not be emulated by U.S. firms (in establishing laboratories in Europe). None of the U.S. companies interviewed was considering such a course.

In contrast, the movement of clinical research abroad should continue for some time. Clearly, the growing sophistication and proliferation of foreign regulatory requirements, the cost advantages of doing such research abroad, and the increasing capability of the medical profession in foreign countries contribute significantly to this movement. At the same time, problems with drug approval mechanisms in the United States have reenforced the attractiveness of foreign clinical research, granted the potential of foreign markets.

Overall, the movement of pharmaceutical technology out of the United States appears significant. In all probability, the pharmaceutical industry transfers more of its stock of technology abroad than other industries. In part, this is natural because the industry is technology intensive and there is a strong economic motive for transferring dosage plants abroad. But a larger cause of this movement of technology abroad is regulatory policies. Perhaps what makes this industry unique is that the most important and effective source of pressure for the movement of technology abroad is not the potential recipients of the technology. Rather, it is the country where the technology is developed, which could, under a set of different policies, derive appreciable economic benefit by not forcing this technology abroad.

Commentary

Edwin Mansfield

During the past several years, Henry Grabowski, working alone and in collaboration with John Vernon and others, has produced a considerable body of research on the effects of regulation on the rate and direction of technological change in the pharmaceutical industry. In this paper he uses data on new chemical entities introduced in the United States, the United Kingdom, France, and Germany, to conclude that since 1962 the United States has shifted from leading to lagging the United Kingdom and Germany. Further, he concludes that the lag with Europe is not confined to drugs with modest or insignificant medical gain but includes important therapeutic advances as well. Finally, he concludes that there is evidence regulation has been a major factor contributing to this lag.

Grabowski's results are interesting and useful. My purpose in these comments is not to take issue with them but to supplement them and to suggest further work to clarify the interpretation of certain points. To begin with, it should be recognized that the phenomenon Grabowski observes—a reduction in the lag between the date when new technology (developed in the United States) is first introduced here and the date when it is first introduced abroad—is not confined to the pharmaceutical industry. In research that I am carrying out for the National Science Foundation, I have found evidence of this tendency in other industries.[1] Mark Schwartz, in his doctoral dissertation written as part of this project, observed this tendency among semiconductor and plastics innovations.[2] William Davidson and Richard Harrigan obtained similar results in a study of 733 nondrug innovations. For example, they found

---

[1] This work is supported by a grant for studies of "Market Structure, International Technology Transfer, and the Effects on Productivity of the Composition of R&D Expenditures."

[2] Mark Schwartz, "The Imitation and Diffusion of Industrial Innovations," unpublished Ph.D. thesis, University of Pennsylvania, 1978.

that 24 percent of the innovations introduced in 1961–1965 were produced in foreign markets within one year after introduction in the United
States, but 39 percent of those introduced in 1971–1975 were produced
in foreign markets within one year after introduction in the United
States.[3] Jack Baranson, in a study carried out for the U.S. Department
of Labor, concluded that American firms in a variety of high-technology
industries are increasingly likely to release their most recently developed
technologies to foreign enterprises.[4]

The reasons why U.S.-based firms transfer their technology abroad
more quickly now than in the past are incompletely understood. In
some cases the quicker transfer seems to result in part from the
diminution of the technology gap between the United States and other
industrialized countries. According to Baranson and others, foreign
firms and agencies are less willing now to accept older technology, and
U.S.-based firms, feeling they have less in the way of a monopoly of
the newest technology than they have had in the past, are more willing
to make new technologies available.[5] Another important factor seems
to be the tendency for U.S.-based multinational firms to organize for
more effective exploitation of opportunities to use their technologies
abroad. There is a growing tendency for firms to improve their capacity
to assess the profitability of new products and processes on a global
basis. And, as Davidson and Harrigan's data indicate, firms with
globally integrated organizations tend to transfer their technology
abroad more quickly than other types of organizations.[6]

With these findings in mind, I am led to wonder whether some of
the measured reduction in the U.S. lead in pharmaceuticals may not
have resulted from similar factors. In other words, is it not possible
that the U.S. lead, as Grabowski measures it, would have declined to
some extent even without the regulatory factors he emphasizes? Judging
from the behavior of other industries during this same period, we must
consider this possibility. Given that so little is known about the factors
responsible for this decline in other industries, it is hard to see how
Grabowski could include them in his analysis, but perhaps he could
compare the extent to which the U.S. lead in pharmaceuticals has
diminished with the extent to which the U.S. lead in nonregulated

---

[3] William Davidson and Richard Harrigan, "Key Decisions in International
Marketing: Introducing New Products Abroad," *Columbia Journal of World
Business* (Winter 1977).

[4] Jack Baranson, "Technology Exports Can Hurt Us," *Foreign Policy* (Winter
1976–1977).

[5] Ibid.

[6] Davidson and Harrigan, "Key Decisions."

industries has diminished to get some feel for the effect of regulation. Such a comparison, of course, would be subject to many limitations and entail many problems, but it would move toward recognizing the possible effects of factors other than regulation on the size of the U.S. lead.

As Grabowski is well aware, it is very difficult to estimate the extent to which the observed change in the U.S. lead in pharmaceuticals has come about as the result of regulatory factors. To try to derive such an estimate, he uses the regulatory approval time in the United States as an independent variable in his regressions. Although this is an imaginative procedure, it should be viewed with considerable caution. As he points out, there need be little or no relationship between the stringency of regulations and how long it takes to process applications. Moreover, the length of the lag depends on the regulatory stringency in the United States and in the United Kingdom. Thus, even if this variable were entirely adequate as a measure of regulatory stringency in the United States, the regressions might still be misspecified. Indeed, if the stringency of regulation in the United Kingdom changed during the period from 1968 to 1975, this could be one possible reason for the poor performance of this independent variable in those years.

Finally, I would like to call attention to the fact that in recent years considerable controversy has raged over the effects of international technology transfer on the technological position of the United States. Some observers fear that U.S.-based multinational firms, by transferring their technology overseas, reduce our technological lead.[7] An important but seldom recognized point is that, if U.S.-based firms could *not* exploit their new technology overseas, they would not carry out as much research and development; as a result, our technological position might in fact be weakened. According to estimates my colleagues and I obtained from thirty firms, about a 20 percent reduction in R&D expenditures might take place if new technologies could not be exported.[8] This topic is quite relevant to the title of Grabowski's paper because there have been a number of recent proposals that the government impose new regulations on the international transfer of technology. Put differently, FDA regulations of the sort described by Grabowski

---

[7] For an account of this controversy, see Edwin Mansfield, "Technology and Technological Change," in J. Dunning, ed., *Economic Analysis and the Multinational Enterprise* (London: Allen and Unwin 1974). Also see E. Mansfield, J. Rapoport, A. Romeo, E. Villani, S. Wagner, and F. Husic, *The Production and Application of New Industrial Technology* (New York: W. W. Norton, 1977).

[8] Edwin Mansfield, A. Romeo, and S. Wagner, "Foreign Trade and U.S. Research and Development," *Review of Economics and Statistics* (February 1979).

are not the only regulations relevant to the international diffusion of technology.

Let me now turn to Josef Brada's paper. Based on interviews with ten pharmaceutical firms, this paper considers the factors that influence international technology transfer in the pharmaceutical industry. Brada concludes, among other things, that the location of research facilities abroad is often the result of pressure from the host countries and that the movement of clinical research is the result of cost advantages and other factors that should continue to be operative. He believes that the drug approval mechanisms in the United States have also accentuated this tendency. In my comments, I shall focus particular attention on overseas research and development, a topic that has suffered from relative neglect.

To begin with, it is worth pointing out that overseas R&D expenditures by U.S.-based firms have grown to the point of high significance. For example, in the early 1970s, about one-half of the industrial R&D performed in Canada and about one-seventh of the industrial R&D performed in the United Kingdom and West Germany was done by U.S.-based firms.[9] Moreover, the drug industry generally has spent a larger percentage of its R&D dollars overseas than most other industries. In 1975, according to PMA figures, U.S. pharmaceutical firms budgeted about 16 percent of their R&D expenditures to be spent abroad.[10] And, as Clymer has pointed out, because U.S. subsidiaries of foreign-based firms are included in the U.S. R&D total but not in the overseas R&D data, the PMA data underestimate the percentage of U.S.-based firms' R&D expenditures carried out overseas.[11]

My colleagues and I have recently carried out a study (supported by the National Science Foundation) of the size and nature of the overseas R&D activities of fifty-five major U.S.-based manufacturing firms.[12] We found enormous differences among firms in the percent of their R&D expenditures made overseas. To explain these interfirm differences, we constructed a simple econometric model in which the

---

[9] Conference Board, *Overseas Research and Development by U.S. Multinationals, 1966–75* (New York: Conference Board, 1976).

[10] Pharmaceutical Manufacturers Association, *Annual Survey Report, 1974–75* (Washington: PMA, 1975).

[11] Harold Clymer, "The Economic and Regulatory Climate: U.S. and Overseas Trends," in R. Helms, ed., *Drug Development and Marketing* (Washington: American Enterprise Institute, 1975), p. 143 and pp. 148–149.

[12] Edwin Mansfield, D. Teece, and A. Romeo, "Overseas Research and Development by U.S.-Based Firms," *Economica* (May 1979), and E. Mansfield, *Statement to the Senate Commerce Committee concerning International Technology Transfer and Overseas Research and Development*, 1978.

explanatory variables are (1) the percent of the firm's sales that come from abroad, (2) the size of its annual sales, and (3) a dummy variable indicating whether or not the firm is in the pharmaceutical industry. This model can explain about half of the observed interfirm variation in the percentage of R&D expenditures made abroad. As would be expected, this percentage is directly related to the percent of a firm's sales that come from abroad and to the size of the firm's annual sales. When these factors are held constant, the percentage of R&D expenditures abroad is significantly higher among pharmaceutical firms than among other firms in our sample.

According to many observers, one major reason why U.S.-based firms have carried out R&D overseas is that costs have been lower there. However, there has been little information published on the extent of this cost differential and how it has varied over time. To help fill this gap, we obtained from thirty-five firms data on the ratio of the cost of R&D inputs in Europe, Japan, and Canada to those in the United States in 1965, 1970, and 1975. The results indicate a substantial cost differential existed in 1965: on average, the cost of R&D inputs seemed to be about 30 percent lower in Europe, 20 percent lower in Canada, and 40 percent lower in Japan than in the United States. Although there was some increase in R&D costs elsewhere relative to those in the United States during 1965–1970, the cost differential remained quite substantial in 1970.

Between 1970 and 1975, the situation changed dramatically. As a result in part of the depreciation of the dollar relative to other currencies between 1970 and 1975, the cost differential was largely eliminated for many firms. On average, the 1975 cost of R&D inputs was estimated to be about 10 percent lower in Japan and about 5 percent lower in Europe and Canada than in the United States. This helps to explain the fact that the percentage of R&D carried out overseas was expected to increase less rapidly between 1974 and 1980 than in the period before 1974. Because the cost differential between overseas and domestic R&D was smaller, it is understandable that firms would expect the percentage of R&D abroad to grow less rapidly than in earlier years. These data pertain to a variety of industries, not pharmaceuticals alone. The experience in pharmaceuticals may be different, of course, from that of this sample of firms.[13]

In conclusion, I wish Brada had provided a somewhat more

---

[13] For some information on relative costs in the United Kingdom and the United States, see G. Teeling-Smith's paper in J. Cooper, ed., *Regulation, Economics, and Pharmaceutical Innovation* (Washington: American University, 1976).

detailed picture of the ways in which FDA regulations have promoted the location of R&D overseas. On the basis of his account, it is very difficult to judge how important the regulatory factor is, relative to other considerations. I appreciate the difficulties in measuring the effects of regulation, but it would be useful to examine particular cases and to see why the FDA regulations tip the balance toward locating R&D overseas. Also, it would be interesting to obtain some estimates from R&D executives of how much R&D they would do overseas in the absence of these FDA regulations. Further, it would be useful to get some idea from them of the effect of Treasury regulation 1.861–8, which was put into effect in early 1977. According to some observers, this regulation may increase the amount of R&D done overseas.[14]

Klaus von Grebmer

As a European I do not dare to venture any value judgments on drug regulation in the United States. Various sources appear to show, however, that the United States does have the strictest drug regulatory philosophy of any industrialized country. In my contribution to this discussion, which is concentrated on Henry Grabowski's paper, I should like to present some European viewpoints on health policy questions arising in connection with the diffusion of drugs.

Der Spiegel recently published a leading article in which it launched a heavy attack on a large German manufacturer for continuing clinical field trials of the drug Trasolyl. This drug, which the company was testing, contains aprotinin as its active substance and had reduced mortality following traumatic shock by about 50 percent. The firm was accused of behaving unethically on the ground that, instead of giving this drug to all patients without further testing, it was continuing its restricted tests and thus was allowing people to die who might otherwise have been saved.[1]

In a similar case, Anturane—a preparation developed by our company, CIBA-GEIGY, and already registered for the treatment of gout—proved to be capable of reducing by 50 percent the incidence of sudden death after a first heart attack. The independent investigators conducting the trials thought it would not be ethical to continue them without informing the patients involved of these preliminary findings. Nevertheless, although the 50 percent reduction in mortality had been

---

[14] See R. Kaplan, "Tax Policies for R&D and Technological Innovation," Graduate School of Industrial Administration, Carnegie-Mellon University, 1976.

---

[1] *Der Spiegel*, vol. 32 (September 11, 1978), p. 54.

demonstrated on the basis of reliable statistics, we have not yet been able to get the drug registered for this new indication in several countries, including the United States.

These two closely comparable cases illustrate the present drug regulation dilemma: on the one hand, "over-testing" a drug is subject to public criticism, coupled with demands for speedier progress and broader diffusion; on the other, difficulties in registering a tried and tested new indication prevent the drug's broader diffusion. In this context, Henry Grabowski's empirical analysis points the way to rational discussion of the pros and cons of drug regulation. The four markets he has analyzed cover between one-fourth to one-third of the world's drug market, including all the key markets except Japan. His findings thus have an important bearing on further discussions and conclusions about drug diffusion.

Assuming that there is a drug lag of the type to which Grabowski referred, three questions that were beyond the scope of his present analysis strike me as being likely to become of major significance from the health policy standpoint. First, what are the national consequences of the fact that patients in the United States—as he discovered—must wait longer than those in other countries before gaining access to important therapeutic advances? Second, what institution or authority is responsible for examining the social costs of a drug's not being on the market? Third, what are the international repercussions of the strict U.S. "drug regulation philosophy"—its effects on the diffusion of drugs?

There are no simple answers to these questions. Professor Grabowski's paper underlines what I would call the "macro" aspects of drug regulation. But heavily increasing concentration on drug safety requirements is bound to take resources away from innovators in the pharmaceutical industry. Today about 50 percent of the industry's research budget is already being spent on safety research. What Professor Grabowski has described on a national level will therefore have severe feedback repercussions on our companies, which not only will hamper the diffusion of new drugs but also interfere with the process of generating new drugs.

In the long run, moreover, the U.S. "drug regulatory philosophy" could serve as a model for other countries. In certain instances it has in fact already done so. The simple reason is that strict regulation in one country prompts regulatory authorities in other countries to emulate it in order to demonstrate their own "efficiency." Within the European Community, for example, there are already signs of a trend toward harmonizing drug regulation on the basis of the highest common denominator. These international "domino effects" eventually could well lead to a disappearance of the drug lag in the United States because all countries will have adopted the strictest forms of regulation. It might be worthwhile to follow up developments in this direction by repeating Professor Grabowski's study in a few years. And another point not to be forgotten is that the adoption of stricter regulations is to some extent politically attractive because almost all politicians interested in this topic will argue that more regulation means better drugs. The logical implication of this argument is that the country with the biggest drug lag must have the biggest lead in the field of international regulatory measures.

As Professor Mansfield has already mentioned, certain differences exist between European regulatory systems and those in the United States. In Europe, we have more flexible systems in the premarketing phase, but much more regulation in the postmarketing phase (in the realm of price controls for example).[2] If and when the European and American systems become combined, I am afraid that we shall then be faced with strictest regulation in both phases, and if drug regulation is too strict, the results may prove highly undesirable. Innovative competition will diminish. The products of innovative research now available on the market, having finally outlived their patent protection, will then become subject to competition from generics. Or, possibly, only a few new drugs will succeed the products now available, in which case the market will dry up, and research-based companies will be confronted with the problem of meeting increasing safety costs from steadily diminishing returns. Sooner or later a break-even point will be reached at which innovative research dwindles to zero. In the long run, this will cause health care costs to rise: of all the medical therapies available hitherto, pharmaceuticals have shown the highest increases in productivity.[3]

In those disease categories in which drug therapies are most urgently required, such as cancer and cardiovascular diseases, research will have to enter new fields. But, if we want 100 percent safety and security, then—by definition—we will be barred from entering these new fields. There, indeed, may well be an inherent logical contradiction between 100 percent safety and innovation, as well as between very strict regulation and innovation. In other words, excessively strict drug

---

[2] Klaus von Grebmer, *Pharmaceutical Prices: A Continental View* (London: Office of Health Economics, 1978).

[3] Walter P. von Wartburg, "The Role of the Pharmaceutical Industry in Containing Health Care Costs," unpublished manuscript, October 1978.

regulation may impede—and possibly is already impeding—the development of therapies for precisely those diseases in which they are most needed. This perhaps could be one reason why, as Professor Grabowski's investigation showed, the *important* therapeutic drugs in the United States have had longer time lags than the other NCEs investigated.

What astonishes me is that consumer organizations have not yet zeroed in on this major problem. It is true that the consumer may be harmed by "bad" drugs introduced too early on the market, but the consumer also has to suffer the consequences when a "good" drug reaches the market too late. The consumer organizations have so far been campaigning only against the first of these two evils and seem to be quite unaware of the second.

Speaking in medical terms, Grabowski's paper can be likened to an initial diagnosis. It should now be worthwhile to invest some brainpower in the problem of therapy and to try to discover what can be done to improve the present situation. I have no concrete proposals to offer, but I could conceive of ways and means to decrease the volume of premarketing surveillance, while on the other hand there are a number of things that might be done in the product liability field in particular and on the postmarketing plane in general.

Today, we are aware of the fact that excessive reliance is placed on premarketing surveillance, including animal experimentation and all other forms of premarketing measures. Once a substance has squeezed through the bottleneck of these premarketing controls, it can be used at once on a broad scale in general practice. In other words, after it has passed through this bottleneck and successfully overcome the final obstacle of clinical trials, it has free and unfettered range on the medical market.

At least one model exists that would provide for step-by-step introduction of a new drug from the laboratory to the market place. In such a model, the emphasis would be shifted from controls on the drug *before* its introduction to controls remaining in force for some time *after* its introduction.

> An ideal regulatory system, in our view, must permit a new drug to be used in an increasingly large number of individuals who can benefit from its effect in decreasingly sophisticated medical settings, beginning with the research scientist in the laboratory and going towards the family physician in the community.[4]

[4] William M. Wardell, ed., *Controlling the Use of Therapeutic Drugs: An International Comparison* (Washington: American Enterprise Institute, 1978), p. 8.

Such a development, however, would be disastrous if it simply means that postmarketing surveillance would become, not a substitute for the present dominance of premarketing surveillance, but something super-imposed upon it. In that case, postmarketing surveillance, instead of enabling society to benefit from the earlier release of a drug, would only lead to increased controls in an already overcontrolled market. Provided this threat did not materialize, I would suggest that one solution might be the stepwise introduction of a drug, upon which controls would progressively diminish during its lifetime.

My last point is that the pharmaceutical industry tends to blame the drug regulators for being too bureaucratic. I recently had a conversation with a member of the equivalent of the FDA in a large European country. He told me, during discussions in his office, that experts often voiced their doubts that it is really necessary to demand that pharmaceutical companies provide additional test data or other additional material for a special registration. He felt that sometimes his colleagues might in fact be overdoing things. Then, however, he added this comment: "But the companies always come up with the data they are called upon to deliver. They never argue, protest, or ask whether or not the additional data are really necessary." I think, then, one should not attach all the blame to the authorities. People working in the pharmaceutical companies themselves should start debating more intensively the whys and wherefores of what they are doing; they should consider what data they can reasonably be expected to collect and discuss the whole matter with the regulatory authority (if the laws will let them).

To sum up, in the field of drug regulation we should try to move away from the incremental approach in favor of a more synoptic approach, which would include all the disciplines and all the relevant medical, economic, and social aspects of a drug to be introduced. I am sure this approach would enable us to work out a better system than we have at present.

Rolf R. Piekarz

One could claim that I am uniquely qualified—or unqualified—among the speakers and discussants. I am the only one who is not directly involved in research or in regulation, nor am I on the receiving end of regulation in the pharmaceutical industry. Also, being the last discussant has both advantages and disadvantages. One of the major disadvantages is that the previous discussants probably have identified all the major weaknesses of the papers presented. The major advantage is that I have an opportunity to pontificate on more general topics and specifically on current research issues. And that is what I am going to do.

I qualify for this task because my group at the National Science Foundation funds a good deal of research on this topic. As a result, many of the reports pass across my desk. Also, I have an informed staff educating me. This circumstance has enabled me to gather impressions of what has been done and of what remains to be done.

Most of all—and this has been touched upon by both the previous discussants—I believe that what we need now are major advances in producing information relevant to making public policy decisions. We know the regulatory process produces lags and additional costs. But what are the dimensions of the major costs, and what are the benefits from these kinds of regulations? I should say here that I have not run across any really good taxonomy for the costs and the benefits involved. The subject seems to be approached on a piecemeal basis.

Professor Brada, for example, speaks of the reduction of U.S. exports and the location of U.S. production abroad. But he does not define the costs to U.S. output as a result of the regulatory activities. As Professor Mansfield pointed out in his discussion, in order to determine the dimensions of the effects of pharmaceutical regulation, we must isolate them from other influences operating simultaneously. Obviously, too, there are other social costs, such as the delays that result from the regulatory process. What are the increases in the number of deaths and illnesses and the increases in suffering? On the other hand, presumably, regulation has certain benefits in reducing these harmful effects by offering greater assurance of safety and efficacy and by discouraging unnecessary tests of possible drugs.

Among my concerns with these papers is their tendency to lump all "regulation" together and their lack of discussion of the effect of different ways of implementing regulations. Such differences are crucial in attempting to assess policy options. What we have is not so much a binary situation—to have or not to have regulation—but a question of implementing specific procedures and improving specific restrictions. What we need is a better idea of implications and effects of specific forms of implementation.

Finally, there is a good deal of talk about the effect of regulation on the absolute and relative capabilities of the United States to generate and diffuse improved technology and scientific information. What is not clear to me is whether the process as it now exists increases or decreases the amount of useful research output. For example, to what extent would our present regulation, or some other form, or no form, cause research to produce a larger number of more important drugs with major therapeutic gains? And again, do the different forms of regulation or absence of regulation, diminish or extend research capabilities? Regulations may encourage or discourage the use of more effective or innovative research techniques. The relationship between regulation and the process of innovation seems to be unexplored territory. What are the effects of regulations, for example, on the market and training for scientists and medical specialists? And very important from the government point of view—because the government itself funds R&D programs—what does regulation suggest about government funding of research as against industry funding of research?

These are just a sample of the questions policy makers need answered so they can make informed judgments. Though the findings that have been discussed here provide increments of useful information, there is a long way to go before the results presented in these papers can be used in the political decision process.

Part
Two

U.S. Regulatory and Patent Reform:
International Implications
for the Supply of Medicines

Introduction

Carole Kitti

Although the topic of this section covers both regulatory and patent reform, introductory comments (reflecting my particular interests) are on the patent aspects of the proposed drug regulations. Patent reform in particular and the protection of intellectual property in general are not topics that generally attract a great deal of interest. Senator Hart in introducing the last patent reform bill said, "If we were measuring the 'potential boredom rate' of various topics for conversation on a scale of 1 to 100, patents would probably get a 99."[1] This comment, of course, does not apply to the two papers to be presented in this session, perhaps because they discuss the very real problems of one particular industry. Both point out quite clearly some of the trade-offs that must be made in federal regulatory reform—trade-offs among incentives for innovative activity, the monopolistic position allowed by patents, and the avoidance of unnecessary duplication of research efforts.

Unfortunately, there is little strong empirical evidence on the extent to which patents are important incentives for innovation. There are arguments on both sides, and the importance of patents no doubt varies by industry. Empirical work has been hindered by the fact that many inventions can be protected either under federal patent law or under state trade secret law. For example, reports of the relative unimportance of patents in certain industries often appear to assume that legal protection of trade secrets is available.[2] Managers interviewed about their firms' behavior claim that, in the absence of patent protection, they would keep their research findings secret and continue their R&D efforts rather than simply take their competitors' findings (by, for example, hiring away key personnel).

---

[1] Arthur R. Whale, "Patent Law Revision: A Dark Look at S. 2255," *Journal of the Patent Office Society*, vol. 59, no. 3 (March 1977), pp. 162–163.

[2] C. T. Taylor and Z. A. Silberston, *The Economic Impact of the Patent System: A Study of the British Experience* (Cambridge: Cambridge University Press, 1973), p. 210; and Fritz Machlup, "Patents and Inventive Effort," *Science*, vol. 133 (May 12, 1961), p. 1463.

There is some evidence that patents are indeed important in the pharmaceutical industry. A study of the British patent system done by Taylor and Silberston concludes that "the pharmaceutical industry stands alone in the extent of its involvement with the patent system. No other major industry approaches pharmaceuticals in its degree of attachment to patent protection; in no other field have critics of patent monopolies been so severe."[3]

The broader topic of intellectual property protection, including both patents and trade secrets, comes up in considering proposed regulatory reforms for FDA. Senate bill S. 2755 provides for disclosure of the now confidential safety and efficacy data submitted by firms in order to obtain FDA marketing approval for new drugs. In return for this disclosure, the company providing the information will be given a temporary five-year monopoly on its use in the United States. That is, a kind of minor patent would be provided for information that is now kept secret but has some of the characteristics of a public good.

A variant of the disclosure policy is contained in a recommendation made by a staff member of the Senate health subcommittee.[4] This proposal provides that temporary five-year protection not be granted to the newly disclosed safety and efficacy data but rather that the patent holder (and provider of these data) rely on the patent for protection against other manufacturers of the same drug. There appears to be little difference in the protection afforded by these two proposals as long as the remaining legal patent life is longer than five years. The recommendation that protection not be granted to the disclosed data, however, also provides that a second manufacturer who wants to produce the same drug and who is stopped by a patent can seek a declaratory district court judgment on the validity of the patent. The reasons behind the apparent stress on early litigation over patent validity are not known, but one might suspect that it reflects a distrust of patents.

I hope these papers will promote a greater awareness of the importance of intellectual property protection (either patents or secrecy) as an incentive for innovative activity and of the complexities of coordinating different forms of protection in international markets, such as those for pharmaceuticals.

---

[3] Taylor and Silberston, *The Economic Impact*, p. 231.

[4] "Five-Year Exclusivity Out: Patent In With New S. 2755 Proposal," *PMA Newsletter*, vol. 20, no. 33 (August 28, 1978), p. 1.

The Political Economy of Innovation in Drugs and Drug Regulation Reform

Edmund W. Kitch

The purpose of this essay is to examine the political economy of drug innovation and use the findings to evaluate the Drug Regulation Reform Act.[1] Particular emphasis is placed on an overlooked problem—the efficient management of innovational resources. This essay applies some points developed in a more general context to the problems of drug technology.[2]

The Problem of Underinvestment

The traditional political economy of innovation begins with the fact that an innovation can be copied. The copying will keep the innovator from capturing the full social value of his innovation.[3] As a result, investment in innovation will be less than the innovation's anticipated social value. Assuming that firms are (on the average) reliable predictors of the value of innovations, the resulting underinvestment will represent a social loss.

At this point the analysis has generally followed two lines. One line suggests the use of tax revenues to subsidize the process of investment in innovation. The subsidy will increase the amount of investment in innovation toward the socially optimum amount. The more basic and fundamental the innovation, the less the ability of an innovator to capture its returns. The analysis suggests, then, that the more basic the research being undertaken, the higher should be the tax subsidy. Doubtless this analysis has something to do with the generally

---

[1] S. 2755, 95th Congress, 2d session, introduced by Senator Kennedy on February 6, 1978. The bill was not reported out of Committee in the 95th Congress.

[2] See Edmund W. Kitch, "The Nature and Function of the Patent System," *Journal of Law and Economics*, vol. 20 (1977), pp. 265 ff, and American Enterprise Institute Reprint No. 87.

[3] This literature is comprehensively reviewed in Fritz Machlup, *An Economic Review of the Patent System*, Study No. 15 of the Subcommittee on Patents, Trademarks, and Copyrights of the Committee of the Judiciary, United States Senate, 85th Congress, 2d session (1958).

high level of support (at least among intellectuals) for government subsidy of research, particularly of basic research.

For any government subsidy to improve the situation it must be managed with sufficient skill so that the returns are positive. The government subsidy will raise the cost of specialized inputs to the research process (because total end demand for these inputs will rise) and thus reduce the amount of nonsubsidized research that would otherwise occur. If the return from the government subsidy is not sufficiently positive to offset this loss, the subsidy will not improve the situation. If the government is a poor manager (because of inability to separate promising from unpromising projects, to allocate funds in proportion to the promise of projects, or to obtain the appropriate match of project and personnel), the subsidy will not produce a social gain.

The other line that has been followed in analyzing the political economy of innovation is the possible use of a rights system to overcome the problem of underinvestment. The patent scheme, which evolved long before methodical analysis of these problems was undertaken, is considered to be such a system. An inventor is entitled to a patent on his invention, and the patent gives him the right, for a limited time, to keep others from using his invention. The patent solution will not be completely effective because some gains from an invention will fall outside the reach of patent claims. For instance, a patent on a particular compound that reveals therapeutic properties of the compound may suggest to others the possibility that related compounds will also have those properties; but those related compounds will not fall within the patent claim. Generally, however, patents will tend to increase returns to innovation and overcome the underinvestment problem.

The Availability of New Drugs

A patent introduces other problems, however. During the life of the patent, its owner will charge the monopoly price for the patented product. If the critical assumption is made—and in the literature it usually has been made—that other firms could acquire and use this information without cost, then the existence of the patent generates a social loss. Persons who would purchase and use the product if its price were lower and who could be provided the product at no additional cost to anyone (except the inventor) are denied the product. In the case of drugs, it has been common for observers to comment on the high margins of price over manufacturing costs enjoyed by some patented drugs and to bemoan the social loss that the high prices cause.

The dilemma of accommodating the long run and short run in the institutional arrangements governing innovation is evident in the literature on the subject. One suggested solution is for the government to condemn the patents on an innovation when they are issued and then make them available to all without charge.[4] The "reasonable compensation" for the condemnation would reward the innovator, and the government's royalty-free licensing would result in optimum current output. The hitch is computing reasonable compensation. It is difficult enough to value a patent at the outset of the innovation's commercial life, and the problem would be much compounded by a government policy that eliminated a commercial market in patents altogether. There is much reason to fear that such an approach would result in overcompensating relatively unimportant innovations and undercompensating the really important ones. Over time, this skewed compensation pattern would itself skew the pattern of investment toward innovations of little social value.

The use of compulsory licensing has been most extensively explored in the literature.[5] Why compulsory licensing might improve the situation is never clearly specified. What is contemplated is compulsory licensing with a royalty, and the royalty under a compulsory license would have the same effect as any other patent-based output restriction. Proponents of compulsory licensing seem to contemplate a uniform royalty according to some general notion of "industrial equal opportunity." But it is a simple analytic matter to demonstrate that a uniform royalty could be worse than a nonuniform royalty under a great number of quite realistic conditions. A fear of monopoly extension seems to underlie the notion of uniform royalty—a fear that a firm possessing both a patent and the right to determine the terms on which others can use it is able to transmute the patent rights into an industrial monopoly. The mechanism by which this is done has never been spelled out, and in my view, the argument simply confuses a large market share with monopoly.

These ideas from the literature have found their way into the political debate about drugs. Although provisions designed to introduce compulsory licensing were a dominant feature of the early Kefauver

---

[4] Michael Polanyi, "Note on Patent Reform," *Review of Economic Studies*, vol. 11 (1943), pp. 61 ff, proposes a licensing scheme close to this solution.

[5] C. T. Taylor and Z. A. Silberston, *The Economic Impact of the Patent System: A Study of the British Experiment*, Department of Applied Economics Monographs, No. 23 (Cambridge: Cambridge University Press, 1973) is an extended evaluation of compulsory licensing.

73

proposals, the thalidomide episode carried drug legislation off in another direction toward a focus on safety. The government holds the power to confer a compulsory drug license upon itself under the existing statutes and from time to time has made use of this power. And there has been much support for government subsidy for medical research on condition that the fruits of the research are not subject to exclusive appropriation.

Any analysis of the institutions shaping innovation in the drug industry in the United States is greatly complicated by the role of the FDA. Whether to market a new drug product and, indeed, whether to begin human testing on a new drug product are decisions made by the FDA not by the firm seeking the innovation. There is some reason to think that, at least since the early 1960s, the FDA has been more cautious than the firms would have been—although the striking rise in judicial product liability standards would have had many of the effects of the FDA regulation. What is clearer is that the FDA, driven by the logic of its own regulatory needs, has imposed upon the process of research and marketing a set of general procedures and standards that apply to all new drugs but that probably are not optimal for many of them. A firm's flexibility to adopt its own procedures has been lost. Most important, the firm's control of the timing of research and marketing has been handed over to the FDA, whose operations cause delays unrelated to drug-specific cost/benefit relationships.

In a paper written in 1972, I pointed out that the effect of delays in the marketing of new drugs would be to shorten the patent term.[6] Patents in the drug industry traditionally have been granted on the chemical entities at the outset of the search for therapeutic effect. The longer the time between the patent application and the marketing date, the shorter the time remaining to obtain a return on the successful investment. This analysis suggested that one effect of the drug amendments of 1962 would be to reduce the number of new drugs reaching market, a result confirmed by others.[7]

---

[6] Edmund W. Kitch, "The Patent System and the New Drug Application," in Richard L. Landau, ed., *Regulating New Drugs* (Chicago: University of Chicago Center for Policy Study, 1973), pp. 81, 84–86.

[7] Sam Peltzman, "The Benefits and Costs of New Drug Regulation," in Landau, *Regulating New Drugs*, pp. 113 ff; Sam Peltzman, "An Evaluation of Consumer Protection Legislation: The 1962 Drug Amendments," *Journal of Political Economy*, vol. 81, no. 5 (1973), pp. 1049 ff; Sam Peltzman, "The Diffusion of Pharmaceutical Information," in Robert B. Helms, ed., *Drug Development and Marketing* (Washington: American Enterprise Institute, 1975), pp. 15 ff.

The First-Appropriation System

Barzel's essay, "The Optimal Timing of Innovations,"[8] convinced me that the problem of optimal innovation strategy cannot be resolved simply by an equation setting the marginal investment in innovation equal to the marginal social return. It is important to consider the process by which resources are brought to bear on possibilities for innovation, as well as the relationship between inputs and outputs. This point suggests conclusions strikingly at odds with the traditional analysis and raises another set of problems to be confronted by those who would reform the controlling institutions.

In his essay, Barzel pointed out that the exploitation of technological information has much in common with the use of fisheries, public roads, and oil and water pools—they are all resources not subject to the exclusive control of an owner. Under a rule of first appropriation, there will be inefficiently rapid depletion of the resource. It has long been a conventional point of welfare economics that a rule basing ownership upon first use creates an incentive to use the resource at a rate faster than would optimize the social value of the resource. The reason is that each competitor in the race for ownership will have an incentive to move up the time of his use in order to be first, the process continuing until the costs of being first are equal to the value of being first.

If fishermen own a fish only if they catch it, they have incentive to catch it before their neighbors do, even though this will result in fishing at a rate that depletes the stock. No one in the process has an incentive to slow down. Similarly, if the right to drive on a particular public road is conferred in order of arrival, everyone will have an incentive to hurry out onto the road, even though this causes a traffic jam, until traffic slows to the point that the value of being on that road is equal to the gain from using it compared to (say) the next best route. This is true even though the traffic then moves at a rate that reduces the capacity of the road to carry it. In the case of oil, a rule that gives ownership to the first person to pump the oil out gives each owner of land over the pool an incentive to pump as fast as possible, even if the effect is to reduce the total amount of oil that can be extracted and to supply oil to the market in a time pattern that reduces its total social value.

Because technological information is not something that can be physically appropriated like fish, roads, and oil, the analogy is not

---

[8] Yoram Barzel, "Optimal Timing of Innovations," *Review of Economics and Statistics*, vol. 50 (1968), pp. 348 ff.

immediately obvious. The fact that I take "some information" does not mean that you cannot have it too. The fact that I have read Barzel's article does not mean that you cannot read it too. Even if we both read it—and indeed if we both read it with inefficient haste—the article will still be there. Similarly, the fact that one firm is exploring the therapeutic properties of compound X does not mean that another company cannot explore those properties, and it certainly does not mean that if both explore them, the properties, whatever they are, will be used up.

Barzel's point, and the point of the analogy, is more subtle. There are two resources involved in fishing, driving, and pumping oil. One is the object—the fish or whatever—and the other is the resources used to acquire the object. An appropriation system causes those resources to be used at an inefficiently rapid rate. In the case of a fishery, the problem is not only that the fish are depleted at an inefficient rate, but also that the fishing boats are used inefficiently. Because ownership of the object sought is based on speed, there is an overuse of resources that produce speed. The number of boats and the amount of equipment they carry will be inefficiently large in relation to the number of fish. Thirty boats might be the socially efficient way to exploit a fishing ground, but a rule of appropriation might produce a fleet of sixty.

In the area of innovation, the key loss from an appropriation rule is the inefficient deployment of the resources used to locate and develop an innovation. For instance, in drugs, if several firms were competing to be the first to prove that a given chemical entity has a therapeutic effect, under a rule that the first to demonstrate the effect was entitled to market the drug, certain things would happen. Each firm would emphasize speed in its work, even though the most efficient way might be to proceed more slowly. Each firm would have to limit its commitment of funds by the estimate of the value of the product adjusted by the chance that some other firm will be first. And each firm would have to duplicate the work of others because, under such a hypothetical rule, there would be no exclusive rights to the information until the effect had been demonstrated. Firms would tend to crowd their resources into possibilities they considered close to fruition and to duplicate each other's work. Because there would be inefficient allocation of research resources, both over time and over the set of innovation possibilities, the output from the resources used for drug research would be reduced.

This analysis could be used to argue against a patent system, because patents are in fact a first-appropriation system, whose basic rule is that the patent on the invention goes to the first inventor. But such an argument turns on confusion about the meaning of the term invention. In common usage, the term invention has a meaning quite different from its meaning in patent law. When we speak of an inventor's invention in everyday speech, we are thinking of the commercial product that the inventor made possible—Alexander Graham Bell's telephone, Edison's light bulb, Land's polarizer, and so on.

But something can be patented long before it has any commercial feasibility at all. Patents are issued on new chemical entities, not upon a demonstration that they are wonder drugs, but upon a demonstration that they have some possible therapeutic effects. After the patent is applied for, the patent owner can search for information about the therapeutic significance of the entity. With the exclusive right to market the drug, the patent owner is the only one with an incentive to find the drug's effect. The patent will eliminate the race to be first in developing the drug. Thus, patents are issued on the basis of "first results," but the issuance of the patent (indeed, for the most part, the application for the patent) can stop the race to be first.

Patents vs. Trade Secrecy

Without patent rights, the only possible system would be true "first appropriation." The literature has long made this point, but from a different perspective; that is, it is unclear whether a patent system is needed to provide returns on innovation because there are other ways to obtain return from innovation.[9] Returns may accrue from headstart —being the first in the market with a new product and having the opportunity to plan promotion and output—and returns are generated by trade secrecy, which may be of long duration in the case of processes that can be practiced without disclosure to the world at large. The first type is actually a version of the second, because the ability to have a head start in the market turns on the ability of the firm to keep its development projects secret.

Trade secrecy—whether based on legal recognition of trade secret doctrines or on the natural ability of the possessor of information to control its dissemination—is the principal alternative to the patent system. In "The Nature and Function of the Patent System" I compared the two systems in some detail and identified six ways a patent system is superior to a trade secrecy system. One of these—the ability of the patent's owner to control the allocation of resources to its development

---

[9] See Arnold Plant, "The Economic Theory Concerning Patents for Inventions," *Economica*, vol. 1 (1934), pp. 30 ff, reprinted in Arthur Seldon, ed., *Selected Economic Essays and Addresses* (London: Routledge and Kegan, 1974), pp. 35 ff.

without the misincentives caused by competition to appropriate the invention—has already been developed at length here. Two others are of particular importance.

First is the transaction effect, which has long been a commonplace of the applied legal literature but has not been noted in the theoretical literature. To quote from "The Nature and Function of the Patent System,"

> A patent system lowers the cost for the owner of technological information of contracting with other firms possessing complementary information and resources. A firm that has a design for a new product or process needs to be able to obtain financing, knowledge about or use of complementary technology, specialized supplies, and access to markets. Unless the firm already possesses the needed inputs, it must enter into contracts. The practical difficulties of entering into contracts concerning trade secrets are spelled out in the applied legal literature. Disclosure of the secret imperils its value, yet the outsider cannot negotiate until he knows what the secret is. Disclosure under an obligation of confidence strengthens the discloser's legal position but may prove costly to the receiver, who must accept the obligation before he knows the secret. The patent creates a defined set of legal rights known to both parties at the outset of negotiations. And although the patent will seldom disclose the real value of the patent, the owner can disclose such information protected by the scope of the legal monopoly. Indeed, most know-how or trade-secret licensing takes place within the framework of patent rights, the agreement involving both a license of the patent and an undertaking to disclose how to apply the technology efficiently. This reduced transaction cost increases the efficiency with which inventions can be developed.[10]

Second is the fact that the patent system makes it possible for firms to allocate their resources among the set of innovation possibilities in a more efficient manner. A striking problem with trade secrecy is that during the period of secrecy other firms have an incentive to invest in the search for information already known to the firm keeping the secret. This duplicate search is economically wasteful. The patent system provides a way to transmit already known information to other firms.

> A patent system enables firms to signal each other, thus reducing the amount of duplicative investment in innovation. Once a patent has been issued, other firms can learn of the innova-

---

10 Kitch, "The Nature and Function of the Patent System," pp. 265, 277–278.

tive work of the patent holder and redirect their work so as not to duplicate work already done. Indeed, the patent gives its owner an affirmative incentive to seek out firms and inform them of the new technology, even before issuance, if the most efficient and hence patent-value-optimizing way to exploit the invention is to license it. Under a regime of trade secrecy, the competitive firm might never learn of a competitor's processes and would not learn of the technology incorporated in a new product until it was marketed. During this period, the investments made in a search for technology already invented by others is wasted.[11]

To illustrate the shortcomings of trade secrecy, suppose a firm is considering the possibility that a compound will act as an antihistimine. The firm runs a series of tests on animals, finds that the compound causes a serious undesirable side effect, and drops the project. If another company considers the possibility of pursuing the same project, it will not know of the first company's negative results and will be led to repeat the same tests to obtain the same information. But if there had been a patent issued on the compound, the second company could explore with the owner of the patent the status of work on the compound. This would save the resources involved in repeating the tests. Conversely, if the first company had obtained positive results and did not have a patent, it would not want to publicize its work. If it had a patent, it would want to publicize the positive results in order to increase the value of its patent rights. The information would then become available to others, who could avoid duplicating the work.

Institutional Changes

These points suggest several institutional problems surrounding drug technology development.

Regulation of Research. The points developed here force us to realize that the FDA is regulating the research process. To determine how it does so is an important part of evaluating its regulation overall. The statute does not formally specify that FDA should regulate research; it is modelled on the assumption that firms control their research, and the FDA approves or disapproves. But given the present multistage regulatory process, and given the existence of regulatory queues, the FDA is in fact influencing the time flow of projects, an important part

---

[11] Ibid., p. 278.

of the whole research process. The statute and the regulations do not address this problem. Doubtless in a world of sometimes-practical people, there are ways a firm can inform the FDA of its priorities and the FDA can readjust its timing and resources, but this suggests an awkward, costly, and *sub rosa* process.

The regulatory problem here is particularly difficult because the process of research and development resource allocation should be constantly reiterative—that is, each new piece of information alters the desired portfolio of projects. Adjustments are hard enough for firms to manage, but when there also must be readjustments through the regulatory process, the difficulty becomes staggering. Imagine that a firm has convinced the FDA that drug X is enormously promising for the treatment of an important disease and that therefore its processing should be expedited. Can the firm then persuade the FDA that—in light of information available a month later—some other drug is more urgent now? Research is an exploration of the unknown, yet the regulatory process requires firms to appear consistent in the positions they take.

The administration's reform bill would greatly aggravate these problems. The bill would substantially increase the degree of control the FDA can exercise over the research process. It is a logical response to much of the criticism of the existing regulatory scheme, but that criticism has not considered the problems of regulating the research process. One of the important criticisms of the existing regulatory scheme is that it confronts the FDA with an all-or-nothing choice. Either a drug is approved for general marketing subject to label limitations or it is not approved for marketing. Once it is approved for marketing, the formal regulatory review of safety and efficacy ends—at the very time the commercial sales (much higher in volume than experimental use could ever be) are generating new information of a potential regulatory value. Because the FDA has an all-or-nothing choice, it tends to be highly cautious in saying yes. The suggested solution—adopted in the administration bill—is to give the FDA a much greater range of choices, making possible stages of controlled release with a wide range of cautionary monitoring and information feed-back procedures.[12]

One of the anomalies of the present regulation is that a drug now released for use under labeling for one condition may come to be used for another condition. At this point, the firm that sells the drug has a strong incentive to ignore the second use. If it recognizes the use, it will be open to the charge that it is violating the law by encouraging the

---

[12] See generally, S. 2755, pt. B, sections 105–145, 95th Congress.

use of the drug for a condition in which its use is not permitted. It has little incentive to undertake the research necessary to obtain FDA approval to expand the labeling, because an expansion in labeling may have little effect in enlarging the market. The drug is already being used for the unlabeled condition, and if the existing illicit use is limited, the potential market may be too small to justify the regulatory expense of legitimizing the label.

The solution proposed in the administration bill is to empower the FDA to order firms to do the necessary research.[13] Exactly how one orders a firm to do research is an interesting problem—doubtless the drafters have in mind a combination of threat and grant. How is the FDA to acquire the information necessary to reorder the research priorities of the firm?

The cumulative effect of these provisions would be a great increase in the scope of FDA involvement in allocating resources to research. To evaluate the regulation it is necessary to look at the efficient management of research resources. From this perspective, the advantage of the present system is that it limits the form and number of potential FDA interventions and probably makes the FDA responses more predictable, in part because they are inflexible.

There are various ways of ameliorating the problem of the firm–FDA research interaction. Firms could be permitted to exchange queue positions, to purchase regulatory speed with money, or with chits. Such a system would have to be flexible enough to permit firms to change their designations over time as they obtained new information. Some explicit recognition of the problem's difficulty would itself make it easier for the agency to fashion procedures to deal with it. The prospects for any solution, however, are dim because the whole problem of procedures for allocating regulatory resources (including speed) among items on the regulatory agenda has defied satisfactory resolution.[14] The complex nature of this procedural problem has caused agencies and critics to ignore it. I would not be surprised if a full study of the problem would conclude that the agency should be held to a first-come, first-served principle, with firms given the rights to exchange places in the queue and deal in side payments.

---

[13] Ibid., section 108(h).

[14] One suggestion is to use formal procedures to develop agenda priorities. See, for instance, Recommendation I of the Civil Aeronautics Board Advisory Committee on Procedural Reform, *Report of the Advisory Committee*, vol. 1–4 (December 31, 1975). I served as executive director for that committee. Increased formality in the process of setting priorities diverts resources from the regulatory tasks themselves.

The basic problem is who is to manage the process of research. The present statute adopts a simple-minded model—the firms do the research, and the FDA, with limited and inflexible powers, checks it. The critics have pointed out that the FDA manages poorly because it does not have the range of flexible powers the management job requires. The response is to give the FDA the powers the management job requires, but no attention is paid to figuring out how the FDA is to acquire the personnel skills and information base necessary to exercise these powers. It is quite possible that the FDA as flexible manager will be considerably more wasteful than the firm as manager with the FDA as arbitrary check. If one thinks that the prospects for improvements in drug technology are significant and that the resources for making the improvements are scarce, the wasteful management of these resources is an important problem.

Research Subsidies. Attempts to offset the effects of regulation by increasing the government subsidy of drug regulation hold little promise. Subsidy can increase input, but it cannot affect the relationship between input and output. One could imagine that in place of a research *forcing* power the FDA could be given a research *buying* power. Drug firms are now reluctant to accept public subsidy for their applied research if in exchange for the funding they lose patent protection. The government is reluctant to provide public funds for research on patented chemical entities. The real purpose of the research-forcing power may be to enable the FDA (acting in concert with NIH or other research grant agencies) to use the *threat* of the forcing power to persuade the firms to accept government research subsidies on an open licensing basis.

One of the important problems of government funding of research, particularly without private or government-held patents, is that it reduces the incentives to make the results of that research available. Those who carry out basic research that leads to major discoveries will have an incentive to communicate them since there will be fame (and fortune) flowing from the first publication of significant results. But discoverers of the mundane and of the negative result, without the prospect of gain from the patent system, have no incentive to disseminate the information.

Research-subsidizing institutions have procedures designed to disseminate information to those working in the field and to allocate efforts across the array of perceived prospects in some sensible way. The process of peer review—as it is practiced, for instance, in some of the old-line National Science Foundation subject-matter areas—performs this function. Within NIH, an important part of a research manager's concern is that resources be sensibly dispersed across a field and that the work being funded does not needlessly duplicate the work of others.

But I suspect that communications among programs or sections, and certainly among agencies, are poor and erratic and that the lack of incentive to communicate generates major waste. Who is to know that a Department of Defense project, conducted seven years earlier for the purpose of assaying some potential threat of germ warfare, in fact involved carrying out the very same testing that is now proposed in connection with the cancer-inducing effects of certain organisms? Who has an incentive to tell? And how would grant applicants find out, even if they wanted to? Moreover, if a research-forcing power exists, will not drug firms have an incentive to keep the FDA from finding out that certain therapeutic possibilities exist?

The problem of creating incentives to communicate research results could be solved by giving grantees the right to obtain and exploit any patents resulting from the work. But this would create another dilemma. The grantees would have an incentive to persuade the grantor to fund work they would have done in any case. Government funds would not have increased research at all, then, they would merely have reduced the grantees' expense. At the margin, the costs and incentives for research would remain exactly the same. Even with the FDA having the contemplated research-forcing power and the firms themselves paying for the research, it is hard to believe that the firms will not be able (at a significant cost, of course) to decoy the FDA into ordering or persuading them to perform work they would have otherwise done.

Patent Protection. Attention to the problem of incentives for (and rights in relation to) drug research and particularly incentives for meeting the FDA regulatory requirements is long overdue. The administration bill addresses the problem by providing that the holder of an approved new drug application (NDA) has a five-year exclusive right to the use of the information submitted in support of the NDA.[15]

The provision responds to concerns of the sort I raised in 1972. I pointed out then that the NDA itself was serving as a "minipatent" and providing an incentive to meet the regulatory burden inasmuch as the FDA was treating the information in the NDA as confidential.[16] Any other firm that wanted to market the same drug would have to do the work all over again. I criticized this position on two grounds. First,

---

[15] S. 2755, section 121(b), 95th Congress.
[16] Kitch, "The Patent System and the New Drug Application," pp. 100–104.

83

it is difficult to justify the claim that the information in the NDA specifically developed for use by the FDA and constituting the basis of regulatory action should be a trade secret unavailable to anyone but the applicant.[17] If not a trade secret, the information may be obtained under the freedom of information act. Second, it is wasteful to require a second firm to engage in research whose purpose is to duplicate information already known. I suggested that the NDA might be treated explicitly as an exclusive market right, like a patent, but that the regulatory information in the NDA be made publicly available.

The administration bill moves part way in this direction, but its solution is unsatisfactory because its protection is only against use of the information by another firm in preparing and prosecuting an NDA. This directly creates an incentive for the second firm to duplicate the work of the first. Exactly how the first firm can show that the work of the second firm was not independent is unclear, especially because the most important piece of information for a firm choosing research projects is often the knowledge that something can be done. Incentives in the administration bill are still principally based on the patent system, but the five-year protection period is so short that any advantage conferred on the first firm is quite small. The bill would not adjust the patent term to compensate for the imposed regulatory lag. It does not, for instance, extend the patent term to ten years from the issuance of the NDA or seventeen years, whichever is greater, nor does it do anything about the failure of the patent system to provide patents on the therapeutic properties of drugs, leaving the oddly skewed incentive that favors exploration of the effects of new chemical entities over exploration of the effects of old chemical entities.[18]

World Drug Research. The development of drug technology is an international process. The administration bill and the predecessor statutory schemes are parochial in their focus. The Convention of Paris (1883) has made patents a stable international system—a desirable result because it is as wasteful for an American to duplicate research already done by a German as it is for an American to duplicate research already done by an American. Because of the international character of the patent system, it is common for a single firm to control a drug patent in all major countries outside the Soviet bloc. This puts that firm in a position to coordinate international research efforts.

The regulatory regimes that have emerged in the post-World War II

---

[17] Ibid., pp. 102–103.
[18] Ibid., pp. 86–100.

decades have been national ones, but they have largely left the firms (which are multinational) in control of the research process. The firms have to satisfy different evidentiary burdens and procedures, and their drugs reach the market at different times in different countries, but the timing of the underlying research and the allocation of resources among projects remain in the hands of the firms. Each firm has an incentive to act as a central international point for the collection of information about its drugs.

If the procedures of drug development and marketing are subject to pervasive national regulation, the ability of the firms to act as international coordinators will be impaired. Yet the prospects for effective intergovernmental coordination in the exchange of research information, allocation of resources, and monitoring of experience in use are poor.

Flexibility is an attractive talisman for the extension of administrative power. The present U.S. and international drug regulatory laws have left pharmaceutical firms largely free to plan the process of drug research and development within the framework of the patent incentive, tort liabilities, and regulatory safety constraints. The environment has been one of market reward and market loss, and the patent system has made it possible for firms to space themselves internationally across the technological prospects and to control the intensity and timing of their efforts.

The FDA has slowed the introduction of new drugs into the United States and possibly increased the average safety of those introduced. It has influenced but not controlled the research process itself. An extension of its powers would carry the possibility that research-intensive firms would largely withdraw from the U.S. market or that the FDA would effectively control the world drug research agenda. There is much reason to think the FDA's structure will continually strengthen its zeal for safety—critics say, too much zeal. But there is nothing about the personnel and structure of the FDA to suggest that it can wisely guide the research and development process. The administration bill, drafted in a form that would liberalize the range of FDA regulatory choices, in fact would give the FDA statutory power to guide research but not the wisdom to guide it well.

The Economics of Pharmaceutical Information: International Impacts of U.S. Regulatory Reform

Kenneth W. Clarkson, David L. Ladd, and William MacLeod

Product innovation in the pharmaceutical industries (as in all others) has always involved risks of research, development, marketing, competition, and the entrepreneur's assessment of these risks. Since the Food and Drug Administration (FDA) has been charged with supervision of standards of safety and efficacy, entrepreneurs have necessarily factored into their calculations the additional expense and risk of the FDA process, as well as the competitive advantage against rivals who must take the same course. To enable the FDA to make determinations of safety and efficacy, drug innovators have been required to disclose extensive data, which have, for the most part, been treated confidentially. S.2755 proposes significant changes in the rules of the game, particularly in the way submitted data are treated. In effect, a kind of eminent domain would be asserted, and the information opened to the public and rivals, domestic and foreign. The data would thus become a part of an open-collection library maintained by the FDA. The purpose of this paper is to explore the possible effects of such legal, institutional, and procedural changes upon the incentives and risk-cost assessments for pharmaceutical innovations.

In a society with perfect foresight and costless transactions, it is a waste for more than one enterprise to engage in the production of information. Information conforms to the characteristics of the pure public good—or (to be more precise) the public capital asset. Once it exists, not only can it be consumed without depletion by any number of users at a given time, but it can be both fully consumed today and entirely saved for tomorrow. Yet, the production of the same information is often repeated.

The reason why producers engage in such apparently wasteful activity of their endeavors is well known: to put it in economic terms, knowledge, at the ultimate point of consumption, is no longer a completely public good. In a world of limited foresight and costly transactions, the inventor and the scholar cannot be sure whether they will be beaten to the patent office or publisher. Both can monitor, at a cost, the activities of their competitors and thereby reduce the uncertainty attending the result of their own projects. Neither, however, can erase that uncertainty: other inventors or scholars may not wish to be monitored. At some point, moreover, our inventor or scholar will perceive that the costs of looking further exceed the expected benefit and will return to the laboratory or library, work, and hope.

Moreover, there are incremental costs associated with spreading and using information generated at one source and one time. The frictions of the real world dictate that the expected value of some information is so low, relative to the cost of acquiring it, that generating it anew is more fruitful than trying to find it in storage. "Learning by doing," or in Phillip Nelson's words, discovering the best "experience goods," is an example of rational repetition in generating knowledge.[1]

Information costs can be reduced. The inventor or scholar is aided by librarians, who have adopted indexing systems that simplify information discovery. Static allocative efficiency is promoted when the holder of information makes it available to users, if the cost of transmitting knowledge is less than the cost of re-creating the knowledge transmittal. The more accessible the librarian makes the information under her or his control, the more thoroughly the optimal properties of the pure public good will be realized.

The open, unrestrained, and essentially free distribution of technical information through publication yields a paltry return to the producer of the information, even under protection of copyright. From the standpoint of the public, viewed in the short run, such a method of distribution might be considered ideal, because any significant charge would tend to limit use of the information. But in the long run it is far from ideal, because the producer of the information must either receive a return on investment sufficient to support his efforts or the public will find its source of information cut off. The patent system is the means that makes the necessary return available. Thus, there is a basic conflict between copyright and patent policy—one encourages the dissemination of information and the other imposes a burden on its use. This conflict between the producers and consumers of information has now been brought to the pharmaceutical industry, and it is—in essence—our subject here.

Section I of this paper looks at the Food and Drug Administration (FDA) proposal to establish a library of pharmaceutical information and attempts to explain its rationale. In the second section, we turn our

---

[1] Phillip Nelson, "Information and Consumer Behavior," *Journal of Political Economy*, vol. 78, no. 2 (March/April 1970), pp. 311–329.

attention to the effects of the proposal (as estimated from three sources) and the debate over the significance of the change. The next section presents a model for understanding the domestic and international consequences of the proposal. A number of potential changes in patent, copyright, and trade secret protection are examined in the fourth section, and concluding remarks are given in the fifth.

The Establishment of the FDA's Research Library

That the FDA would grow into the world's leading repository of pharmaceutical research information was a predictable consequence of legislation enacted in the early 1960s. The law's requirement meant that the agency had to know nearly as much as the sponsoring firm about a drug before that drug could be introduced to the general public. By the end of the 1970s, as the pharmaceutical industry and the FDA adapted themselves to numerous legislative and procedural changes, the competitive and clinical importance of the data submitted to the FDA came to be understood.

This time—the end of the 1970s—marked the completion of the second seventeen-year patent generation (1962–1979) since the beginning of the post-World War II pharmaceutical research revolution. The passing of the first generation coincided with the 1962 Kefauver-Harris amendments to the Food, Drug, and Cosmetic Act of 1938. Subtracting one patent life from 1962 reaches back to 1945. At that time, the pharmaceutical industry, invigorated by the successes of penicillin and the sulfa drugs, directed its efforts toward creating new drugs for an expanding consumer economy. The 1940s and 1950s witnessed a sustained parade of unique and valuable products, proliferating under the protection of patents, contributing to a period of unprecedented profitability for drug firms and unprecedented improvement in general health. The commercial monopolies attained by the new drugs sometimes waned as molecular refinements were brought to the market by competitors. The drugs that reached the marketplace in 1945 and thereafter emerged under patent protection lasting until nearly 1962. This was important: the technological and financial requirements for commencing the manufacture of drugs were relatively modest at the time, measured against expected revenues from the new products.

During the 1960s, pharmaceutical products surviving the earlier competition in drugs came out from behind their patent shields, some of them still in prominent market positions. The temporary patent monopolies neared their end, the products moved toward the public domain, and the onset of competition was imminent. There remained, however, a question of policy regarding the mechanism by which competition would be permitted. The answer was ultimately provided by the Abbreviated New Drug Application (ANDA) procedure. By that procedure, a manufacturer proposing to introduce a generic copy of an approved drug already on the market need not go through the elaborate testing procedures required of new drugs. Instead, the latecomer's obligation under the Food, Drug, and Cosmetic Act is met by supplying FDA with information and tests to demonstrate that the proposed commercial drug is chemically equivalent to the original brand and that the manufacturing practices to be used would meet FDA standards. Simple reference to established literature on the safety and efficacy of the drug would suffice to meet those criteria for approval of the new drug application.

But because of the FDA's interpretation of the term *new drug*, the ANDA is available for copies of *pre*-1962 drugs only. That term creates FDA's authority to regulate compounds meeting the definition. A new drug is defined as "any drug the composition of which is such that such drug is not generally recognized, among experts qualified to evaluate the safety and effectiveness of drugs, as safe and effective for use under the conditions prescribed . . . in the labeling thereof."[2] The addition of the effectiveness requirement contributed most heavily to the impact of the 1962 amendments on the development of new drugs. But the definition of "new drug," still lacking any reference to age or time, did not change. All drugs, including those prescribed for years, were potentially new drugs under the law because their effectiveness had not been previously certified by the FDA. Pharmaceuticals that had been introduced before 1962 were reassessed in a comprehensive review by a committee of experts operating under the aegis of the National Academy of Sciences and the National Research Council (NAS-NRC). This review resulted in the withdrawal of many drugs and requirements for further listing of others.[3] Because these experts fit the description in the act ("experts qualified to evaluate"), presumably their recognition of an effective drug meant it was no longer "new" and therefore that it was exempt from the strict requirements of the New Drug Application (NDA) set up by the 1962 amendments. Thus, the expiration of the patent for a profitable drug ushered in the filing of ANDAs with the FDA, the approval of which would signal direct competition with the original entity. By the ANDA procedure, the FDA effectively re-

---

[2] 21 U.S.C., section 321(p).

[3] See *Federal Register*, various issues (1966–1970) for lists of approved drugs. These "reapproved" new drugs then qualified for the ANDA.

duced a serious barrier to potential competition (a barrier the FDA had itself erected).

For drugs introduced under the amended law, the picture changed. The FDA dissolved its group of advising experts when the experts had finished evaluations of pre-1962 drugs. For drugs from 1962 and after, the FDA itself undertook to evaluate efficacy claims. The agency did not accord itself the same status it accorded to the NAS-NRC, however. Approval of new drug applications by the FDA after 1962 (approval implying that the supporting evidence substantiated claims of efficacy) did not constitute "general recognition" by experts required by the act. Thus, 1962 became the dividing line between "old" and "new," and a new drug could remain a new drug indefinitely, despite a valid NDA on file.

Irony can be seen in the disparity between standards of evaluation employed by the FDA and those used by NAS-NRC: FDA has been the tougher judge. Nonetheless, for a generic competitor to gain permission to market a copy of a post-1962 drug, the requirements would be essentially the same (except for antibiotics) as they had been for the innovator. As Edmund Kitch noted in 1973, the increasingly expensive NDA might have become a perpetual patent by raising the cost of entry into a product market to the point that few drugs would be challenged, patent or not.[4]

The typical new drug enjoyed the protection of a patent as well as the NDA barrier. Thus the "NDA as patent" was largely hypothetical for most products in 1973.[5] But this will cease to be the case as the first post-amendment drugs outgrow their patent life. Unless there is a change in FDA policy, a growing number of drugs will be on the market with expired patents but without competitors. Given the political environment in which the FDA must operate, and the passions aroused by the subject of drug prices, one would expect a reappraisal within the agency. One possible change would be to permit the release of safety and efficacy information that the innovator supplies upon filing of the original NDA. These data, combined with the recognition and acceptance encouraged by their release, could then be used in support of subsequent applications by competitors.

The relevant section of the proposed legislation, S.2755, is Section

---

[4] Edmund W. Kitch, "The Patent System and the NDA," in Richard Landau, ed., *Regulating New Drugs* (Chicago: The University of Chicago Center for Policy Studies, 1973), p. 106.

[5] In practice, the FDA has been approving some follow-on NDAs without requiring the full safety and efficacy complement, but admits that it is treading on uncertain legal grounds in doing so.

111.[6] This section sets out the necessary contents of a petition to obtain a drug monograph (the proposed reincarnation of the NDA) and indicates which of the contents will be made public. Although Senator Kennedy reports that the origin of the bill was an interdisciplinary staff of experts from Congress, FDA, and industry, convened in December 1977,[7] the provisions relating to public disclosure had their origin in the FDA. Prior to that time, the FDA, independently, had already been considering the feasibility of such a proposal.[8]

The FDA's concern with confidentiality was twofold. Secrecy prevents informed public participation in the drug approval process and thus removes a check against abuse of administrative discretion. The agency also believes that secrecy leads to needless duplication of testing, which not only wastes resources but also exposes test subjects to unnecessary risks during the experiments. Addressing this concern, S.2755 provides for public disclosure of three reports submitted in the monograph: (1) summary of investigations deemed adequate to disclose the basis for concluding that the drug is safe and effective; (2) detailed description of all investigations, containing the protocols, tables, compilations, and analyses of all data and information relevant to safety and efficacy; and (3) full report of all data and information from all investigations.[9] Dis-

---

[6] S.2755, 95th Cong., 2d sess., March 16, 1978.

[7] *Congressional Record* (Senate), p. S.3873, March 16, 1978.

[8] See, for example, Richard Crout, "New Drug Regulation and Its Impact on Innovation," in Samuel Mitchell and Emory Link, eds., *Impact of Public Policy on Drug Innovation and Pricing* (Washington: The American University, 1976), pp. 254–260, in which the monograph system with the release of data was outlined; and Pracon, Incorporated, *Study to Assess Impacts of Releasing Safety and Effectiveness Data on the Pharmaceutical Industry's Incentives to Invest in and Conduct Research and Development Programs* (Washington: Food and Drug Administration, January 1978).

[9] Section 111(b) Petitions Regarding a Monograph—
(1) A petition to issue a monograph for a drug entry shall contain the following: . . .
(B) Three reports . . . of evidence derived from all investigations that have been made to evaluate the effectiveness of the drug entity and to assess its risks, as follows:
(i) A report in summary form of (I) each such investigation, and (II) data and information from such investigations. Such summary shall be adequate to disclose the basis on which the petitioner concludes that the drug entity is effective and has been assessed for risks.
(ii) A report containing (I) a detailed description of each such investigation, (II) the protocols for each such investigation, and (III) tables, compilations, and analyses of all data and information obtained from each such investigation and relevant to the evaluation of the effectiveness of the drug entity and the assessment of its risks.
(iii) A full report of all data and information from each such investigation.
Section 111(j) Disclosure of Reports Contained in a Petition—(continued on p. 92)

closure of the first report would be made upon filing of the petition, and the report would be available to all interested parties. The more detailed second and third reports would also be made available but only to parties with no commercial interest in the information. People interested in participating in hearings on the monograph would be allowed to view the monograph but not to copy the data. When the monograph is issued (the new drug approved), the latter two reports would be released to any interested party, commercial representatives included.[10]

The FDA recognizes that these measures could have a detrimental impact on research investment in the drug industry. Following "economic impact" directives, the FDA commissioned two economic studies—one by an outside consultant,[11] the other in-house[12]—to estimate the impact on research and development. Only one of the analysts reached a definite conclusion: the full disclosure of safety and efficacy data would decrease U.S. pharmaceutical industries' expenditures on R&D by $56 million annually, or up to 4.7 percent of total R&D.[13] As would be expected, the assumptions on which the study was based have been the subject of debate.

Of the FDA's two goals in proposing the release of research information—public participation and more efficient research—it was believed only the latter involved potentially significant economic costs. Drug innovation would decline as a result of falling revenues and reduced research efforts by innovators losing sales to less progressive competitors. This economic proposition already had been the subject of extensive research. The proposals, then, offered the perfect opportunity for the FDA to marshal the results of that work in support of its position.

---

(2)(A) Upon the filing of a petition . . . the report in the petition described in subsection (b)(1)(B)(i) shall be available to the public.

(B) Except as provided in Paragraph (3), the reports in a petition described in clauses (ii) and (iii) of subsection (b)(1)(B) shall not be available to the public until the date the Secretary issues or amends the monograph with respect to which the petition was filed. On and after such date such reports (other than any matter in such reports which is described in section 552(b)(6) of title 5, United States Code) shall be available to the public.

(3) Upon the filing of a petition . . . the reports in the petition described in clauses (ii) and (iii) of subsection (b)(i)(B) may be disclosed to, but not copied by, any person who . . . [satisfies the Secretary that he will not use them for commercial purposes] (Footnotes omitted)

[10] S.2755, section 101(2).

[11] Pracon, *Study to Assess Impacts of Releasing Safety and Effectiveness Data.*

[12] Fay Dworkin, "Impact of Disclosure of Safety and Efficacy Data on Expenditures for Pharmaceutical Research and Development," mimeographed (Washington: Food and Drug Administration, April 1978).

[13] Ibid., p. 17.

The Methodology and Findings of the FDA Economic Studies

The first step in determining the effect of a policy change on industrial research and development is to *identify the determinants of the R&D budget*. In the economic literature, there is authority for the proposition that firm sales (or related financial data) account for most of the variation in R&D funding, at least for the regulatory period in the past.[14] This proposition, essentially a supply model for R&D, was verified by the FDA's studies, which found that about two-thirds of the pharmaceutical R&D budget was thus explained.[15] Because revenue from sales is measurable, a simple model could be constructed that relates a policy change to the effect on R&D through the medium of funds available for that purpose. Accordingly (the logic went), the release of safety and efficacy data would expose sales of the research-intensive firms to the risk of encroachment by less research-intensive firms. The extent of risk was determined by the magnitude of innovators' sales susceptible to data availability and not protected by patents. The loss of investment in R&D, as sales were transferred to the less research-intensive firms, would be the difference between the amounts each sector devotes to R&D. Because pharmaceuticals are distributed internationally, estimates were made of the strength of patent protection in both domestic and foreign markets, of the significance of U.S. data in gaining new drug approval by the relevant regulatory authority, and of the amount of sales rendered vulnerable by the availability of the data.

The FDA distinguished potential gainers and losers by their respective investments in R&D.[16] From a sample of forty-nine Pharmaceutical Manufacturers Association (PMA) members, firms were placed in the intensive category if their 1975 R&D expenditures exceeded $10 million. The others were classified as less research intensive. The study assumed that innovators were in the research-intensive category, and they would lose sales to the follower firms—those in the weaker research class—if the latter were able to use safety and efficacy data to support applications for competitive drugs. If no aggregate quantity or price changes followed the new competition, revenue losses would equal gains and the net effect could be determined by calculating how funds

---

[14] For a discussion of these issues, see Erol Caglarcan, Richard E. Faust, and Jerome Schnee, "Resource Allocation in Pharmaceutical Research and Development," in Mitchell and Link, *Impact of Public Policy*, pp. 337–339.

[15] Pracon, *Study to Assess Impacts of Releasing Safety and Effectiveness Data*, p. 61.

[16] Dworkin, "Impact of Disclosure of Safety and Efficacy Data," p. 5.

would be reallocated to R&D when sales were transferred from the intensive-research to the less-intensive-research sector.

To determine the amount of revenue transfer, it is necessary to isolate those sales not protected by patent—a percentage of total sales that will, of course, vary among countries according to their respective patent laws. For the U.S. market, 1975 sales of prescription drugs were broken down to show the proportion of all sales taken by drugs introduced since 1940 and by unpatented drugs introduced since 1962. It was found that approximately 50 percent of the estimated $7.4 billion in domestic drug sales in 1975 came from post-1940 drugs. Of this portion, 14.2 percent came from sales of unpatented post-1962 drugs. For simplicity, the study assumed that foreign sales were also split in half between sales of drugs introduced before and after 1940, although patent protection percentages would be expected to differ.[17]

Table 1 summarizes the data, showing the value of sales of new drugs at risk (unpatented), obtained for domestic markets by taking 14.2 percent of the new drug sales, the portion without patent protection. The estimates for foreign sales at risk were determined in three stages. First, the level of patent protection was noted to find whether generic competition would be prevented regardless of the extra data supporting a new drug.[18] Second, the acceptability of test data was checked; if the foreign country would not accept unpublished U.S. data, then the fact that it was available from the FDA would cause no change. Third, if the foreign country accepted U.S. data, then the strictness of its review was checked to determine whether the additional information released by the FDA was redundant, and consequently unnecessary for approval.

Market share figures for U.S. firms were available for only the top nine foreign markets. These markets did, however, account for 66 percent of the firms' foreign volume. Of the $3.7 billion in sales in these nine markets, $980 million was found to be vulnerable to new competition. The greatest probable impact would be on the Canadian market, where patent protection is weaker and foreign data are acceptable.[19]

---

[17] Ibid., pp. 11–16.

[18] The extent of patent protection for pharmaceuticals can vary from full product and process protection to no coverage at all. Some countries protect only the drug product itself. Others protect the process for manufacturing it, which is more easily circumvented.

[19] Canadian patent law protects only the process of manufacturing, not the product itself. However, Canadian authorities suggested that the U.S. policy change could encourage them to require local data. A preference for locally performed tests can come about for two reasons: first, different national populations may have different reactions to certain agents (although empirical evidence on this is weak); and second, independent agencies may see some value in repeating tests in the fashion required by their rules.

TABLE 1

ESTIMATED ETHICAL PHARMACEUTICAL SALES OF NEW DRUGS AND OTHER DRUGS BY U.S. FIRMS IN DOMESTIC AND FOREIGN MARKETS, AND SALES AT RISK, 1975

(millions of dollars)

Market	Sales by all U.S. Firms	Research-Intensive Firms				Non-Research-Intensive Firms			
		Total	New drugs (1940+)	New drugs at risk	Estimated shift in sales	Total	New drugs (1940+)	New drugs at risk	Estimated shift in sales
Domestic	7,387	6,574	3,287	467	51	812	406	58	0[a]
Foreign	4,796	4,268	2,134	711	553[b]	528	264	88	66
Total	12,183	10,842	5,421	1,178	604	1,340	670	146	66

[a] Any losses will be captured by similar firms, leaving no net effect.

[b] $533 million to foreign firms plus $20 million to all firms.

SOURCE: F. Dworkin, "Impact of Disclosure of Safety and Efficacy Data on Expenditures for Pharmaceutical Research and Development," mimeographed (Washington: Food and Drug Administration, 1978), pp. 11–16.

Possible effects were noted in West Germany and Spain, whose markets increased the figure to $980 million. A rough estimate for the remaining markets was obtained by grouping them according to degree of patent protection, which yielded a likely impact on 50 percent of their total sales. Adding this 50 percent brings the total foreign sales exposed to increased competition to $1.9 billion.

The final step, estimating the share of the vulnerable sales that would be picked up by the followers, involved sensitivity analysis to show the loss for different degrees of encroachment by rivals. Ranges were thus obtained for the impact of data release on sales and R&D, the limits depending on market captures ranging from approximately 10 percent total—foreign and domestic—to nearly 100 percent in each sector. The assumption that all sales in question were transferred to follower firms brought the revenue estimate to the neighborhood of $1.2 billion, with the R&D investment loss rising to $90 million. The final estimate was put at about one-half these levels. Assuming that follower firms could capture no more of the new drug markets than they now hold in all drugs, they would be able to absorb $670 million in converted sales, yielding a final R&D decline of $56.5 million, or 4.7 percent of total 1976 outlays.[20]

In the debates that followed the announcement of the proposed regulations, analysts came forward with various estimates of their impact. Representatives from industry and government presented pictures that varied primarily according to the differences in assumptions. The lack of agreement prompted FDA Commissioner Kennedy's statement that the potential impact of the law depends on whose judgments of the state of the foreign regulatory world one accepts.[21] Not surprisingly, the state of the foreign regulatory world appeared more threatening to analysts from industrial settings than to policy makers within the FDA.

Table 2 presents data on U.S. sales in various world markets and compares this with IFPMA and FDA estimates of those sales vulnerable to release of safety and efficacy data. While there has been disagreement over the potential impact of data release, the range of estimates runs from $296 million to $3,090 million. The highest sales figures indicate the maximum loss to the innovative firms, if noninnovative com-

---

[20] Dworkin, "Impact of Disclosure of Safety and Efficacy Data," p. 18.

[21] FDA, "Supplemental Analysis of the Impact of Provision in S. 2755 Regarding Disclosure of Safety and Effectiveness Data on Foreign Markets of U.S. Multinational Firms," Tab C of enclosure to letter from the Director of FDA's Office of Legislative Services to members of Senate Subcommittee on Health and Scientific Resources and House Subcommittee on Health and Environment (June 16, 1978), p. 1.

TABLE 2

VULNERABLE U.S. SALES COMPARED WITH WORLD MARKETS, 1976

(millions of U.S. dollars)

World Market for U.S. Pharmaceuticals	Total Pharmaceuticals Sales[a]	Percent of World Market	U.S. Firms' Share (Percent)	Estimated U.S. Sales in Each Country[b]	Estimated Maximum Vulnerable Sales from Release of Data
United States	7,550	17.7	84.0	6,342	296[c]
Japan	5,360	12.5	12.2	654	0
West Germany	3,360	7.9	12.6	423	423
France	2,880	6.7	17.4	501	0
Italy	2,000	4.7	15.8	316	0
Spain	1,300	3.0	14.4	187	187
Brazil	1,200	2.8	35.4	425	425
United Kingdom	970	2.3	38.4	372	0
Mexico	935	2.2	49.6	464	464
Canada	580	1.4	63.4	368	368
10 market total[d]	26,135	61.2	38.5	10,052	2,163
Other[e]	16,565	38.8	11.2	1,854	927
World total[d]	42,700	100.0	27.9	11,906	3,090

[a] 1976 estimated data. [b] Derived by applying U.S. firms' share to total dollar sales.
[c] Authors' estimate of U.S. vulnerable sales based on the reduction in present value of drugs that lose patent protection after five years.
[d] Includes United States. [e] Includes about 150 other nations, including some third world countries.
SOURCE: FDA, "Supplemental Analysis of the Impact of Provision in S. 2755 Regarding Disclosure of Safety and Effectiveness Data on Foreign Markets of U.S. Multinational Firms," Tab C of enclosure to letter from the Director of FDA's Office of Legislative Services to members of Senate Subcommittee on Health and Scientific Resources and House Subcommittee on Health and Environment (June 16, 1978), Charts 1–3.

petitors manage to appropriate 100 percent of the exposed markets. These revenues are merely transferred from firm to firm within the industry, but the important question from the standpoint of drug consumers is the effect such shifts would have on the output of new drugs. This effect can be derived by taking the percentage of the transferred sales that would have been devoted to R&D had they remained with the innovative firms.[22] At a research-to-sales ratio of 9 percent, the investment loss falls in the range from $26.6 million to $278 million. Thus, the potential shortfall could be over 3 percent of U.S. sales or more than 20 percent of the $1.2 billion that U.S. firms spent on R&D in 1976.

If the relationship between funds devoted to industrial R&D and the output of the R&D process remains relatively stable throughout the shift in revenues, then there is sufficient information here for the FDA to reach a policy decision. The trade-off is between a decrease of something less than 20 percent in the flow of new pharmaceuticals and an increase in the efficiency of the use of information generated in the development process.

The International Market for Pharmaceutical Innovations

Models of innovation based on financial supply theories have never held a comfortable position in economic theory. Economic reasoning suggests that capital markets are available to the entrepreneur wishing to produce a valuable good or service. But with innovation in the pharmaceutical industry, as with innovation generally, arguments exist that tend to support internal financing. Investment in research and development is risky, but it is not risk alone that distinguishes R&D from many other activities financed by external sources. Pharmaceutical innovation presents the problems of forecasting and assessing the scientific or medical risks (as well as the market or commercial risks) of an R&D program and communicating them to potential outside supporters. Individual research divisions in the industry enjoy productive streaks and suffer dry stretches. The courses, and varying productivities of research are difficult to predict from within the firm, let alone from outside. Aggregate industry data that suggest a relatively stable relation-

---

[22] Alternatively, if prices are forced down to marginal production costs by the increase in competition, then the follower firms need not acquire the entire market in order to eliminate profits on the innovative drug. It is the surplus of price over marginal cost, providing funds for R&D, that is the relevant variable in the analysis.

ship between resources contributed and innovations produced in the development process show a statistical smoothing and mask the irregularity, variability, and risks for the individual firm.

These considerations have lent some credibility to a supply model of pharmaceutical innovation. There is, however, another factor that brings attention to that same side of the innovation equation. Virtually all important changes experienced within the industry during the last twenty years have affected the supply of new drugs more than the demand for them. The major regulatory initiatives—requirements of proof and efficacy, stricter standards for new drug approval, the IND process—have affected the costs of innovating.

During the 1940s and 1950s, when the United States was the undisputed world leader in pharmaceutical innovation, the costs of reforms would be borne in the United States and the benefits to accrue from them enjoyed there. The country insulated its markets by regulation from potentially dangerous products that might be developed locally or imported from abroad. Thus, purely domestic analysis seemed appropriate. The shortcomings of this analysis began to gain recognition as observers noted the growing international scope of the industry and the declining role played by plants located in the United States. In 1955, about 40 percent of international shipments of pharmaceutical products from the ten largest exporting countries originated in this country. During the next twelve years, the U.S. share dropped to less than 20 percent. The nine foreign countries increased their exports by 250 percent, compared with the U.S. growth of only 26 percent. This trend continued into the 1970s.[23]

The increasing importance of foreign sources of pharmaceuticals was not a reflection of an absolute decline for U.S. companies. Rather, it indicated the limited expansion of the domestic operations of the U.S. firms as they began to invest elsewhere. Between 1965 and 1975, the proportion of foreign sales to total revenues of PMA member firms increased from 25 percent to an estimated 46 percent.[24] As Harold Clymer noted in 1975, sales in Europe and Japan had been expanding for ten

---

[23] David Kay et al., "The International Regulation of Pharmaceutical Drugs," unpublished report (Washington: The American Society of International Law, 1975).

[24] Harold Clymer, "The Economic and Regulatory Climate: U.S. and Overseas Trends," in Robert Helms, ed., *Drug Development and Marketing* (Washington: American Enterprise Institute, 1975), p. 143, and Table 2, column 4. These figures are low estimates because the presence of some foreign subsidiaries in the U.S. sample inflates domestic sales. The actual ratio has probably exceeded 50 percent.

years at twice the rate of sales in the United States.[25] Expenditures by the industry overseas (an indication of movements of manufacturing resources) were outstripping those in the United States by factors of four and five to one. As a result of these trends, major pharmaceutical firms now have plants in several foreign locations,[26] and expenditures on research and development have shifted similarly.

Different explanations have been sought for the declining prominence of the United States as a base for the industry's operations. The leading suspect has been increasingly demanding FDA regulation. There are other causes, however, including the companies' desire to be near growing markets and the preferences in other countries for locally researched and produced drugs. We do not assess here the various explanations or their relative force. Our point is that the very idea of the "United States pharmaceutical industry" is growing obsolete. The United States is gradually becoming another market in which the international pharmaceutical industry conducts its business. It is no longer sufficient to look only at the impact of U.S. policy on the aggregate operations of the domestic industry, because the viability of the industry and its operations in the United States have grown increasingly independent. Studies assessing the consequences of any government policy must account for both the effect on the industry *and also* the effect on its operations in the affected market. The effects may be quite different.

Graphic illustrations of this point have been provided in the debates over the so-called drug lag, said to occur when drug introductions overseas precede by years the introductions of identical drugs in U.S. markets.[27] The drug lag demonstrated that pharmaceutical innovation, although affected by U.S. policy, did not suffer worldwide to the same extent it did in the United States. In addition to adjusting to the regulatory climate at home, U.S. drug producers began to direct research efforts overseas, and advances followed these efforts. According to Clymer, ". . . the giving of priority to foreign markets has increased the tendency to carry out development and initial clinical investigations of

---

[25] Clymer, "Economic and Regulatory Climate," p. 145.

[26] For example, the latest annual reports show Eli Lilly and Company with manufacturing and sales facilities in seventeen foreign countries, sales staffs in forty-two more; Merck & Co. with plants in twenty-seven other countries, research laboratories in four; SmithKline Corporation with manufacturing facilities in seventeen, research in nine; and the Upjohn Company with twenty-six manufacturing and eight research facilities overseas.

[27] See, for a review of this development, William Wardell and Louis Lasagna, *Regulation and Drug Development* (Washington: American Enterprise Institute, 1975).

new therapeutic agents in the market where product introduction is likely first to take place."[28]

How much priority is given to foreign markets is crucial: that will determine the extent to which firms in the international industry seek to adjust to the requirements of one individual nation, instead of seeking environments more conducive to research and production. One measure of foreign importance we have noted is the share of PMA-member drug sales that are consummated overseas—nearly half in 1976. It was on the basis of overseas sales figures that the earlier policy studies determined the risk to the drug industry if safety and efficacy data were to be released. This yielded the estimates summarized in Table 2. These data, within limits, *do* reveal the current industry sales that would be jeopardized by the proposed revisions and suggest a significant financial impact. They do *not*, however, indicate the importance of foreign markets for the future sales of new pharmaceuticals; and it is this latter factor that ultimately will determine the direction of pharmaceutical innovation. The data presented so far show only the way the supply of resources available to domestic progressive firms may be affected by the policy—not the way prospective revenues generated by new entities may be altered. That depends on the future sales of new drugs. Those future sales are not likely to follow current patterns of market concentration.

In fact, the most recent available estimates do not provide an accurate picture even of current market shares held by the many firms in different countries, inasmuch as the composition of pharmaceutical markets is always in flux. This characteristic of pharmaceutical competition has been recognized and documented by Douglas Cocks for domestic markets.[29] Between 1962 and 1972, all but five of the twenty-one largest pharmaceutical firms in the United States experienced market share displacements sufficient to change their size ranks. The average change in rank was more than four positions. Cocks found that a significant cause for the change was the success of individual research efforts in introducing new drugs. The firms that maintained or improved their market ranks were the ones that had outperformed their competitors' innovative efforts. The firms that dropped had relatively unproductive laboratories.[30] It is evident that the relatively short

---

[28] Clymer, "Economic and Regulatory Climate," p. 152.

[29] Douglas Cocks, "Product Innovation and the Dynamic Elements of Competition in the Ethical Pharmaceutical Industry," in Helms, *Drug Development and Marketing*, p. 225.

[30] Ibid., pp. 242–246.

commercial life of pharmaceuticals makes them an unreliable source of continued market dominance.[31]

Pharmaceutical companies maintain a diversified portfolio of research activities and drugs. Overall sales (which may be relatively stable) do not reveal the dramatic shifts that take place within separate therapeutic categories. A significant new chemical entity can establish itself as a major market leader in a relatively brief interval. Cocks shows two graphic examples where 1971 market leaders in antihypertensives and psychopharmaceuticals were unknown eight years before.[32] The therapeutic value of an innovation and the size of its prospective market determine its expected revenues. Whether a particular firm was dominant in a given category in the past may have little to do with its future prospects.

The innovative pharmaceutical firm would pay close attention to the vulnerability of its existing sales, but a more relevant concern would be the ways in which the profitability of current expenditures on research and development might be affected by a change in U.S. policy. The most important question concerning the industry's performance in the United States is not the amount of existing sales placed at risk, but the amount of future sales jeopardized. Only if past sales are representative of future sales are we justified in basing predictions on existing levels of market penetration, and experience provides no support for such an assumption. Indeed, the continued migration of resources and revenues from the United States to foreign countries suggests the opposite. To expect current levels to persist in various markets would be to imply, for example, that a new drug introduced by a U.S. firm in both Great Britain and the United States would capture 38 percent of the British market and 84 percent of the domestic market, because those ratios have held recently. The more likely result would be roughly equal penetration in each market in which a drug is introduced. The drug of choice in one country for a particular indication is likely to become a significant treatment wherever it is offered.

Present levels of foreign penetration into local markets are, of course, remnants of the past. Like balance sheets, they reflect the consequences of prior events. The fact that the reflections are changing

---

[31] The Pracon study found a median of three years between the introduction of an innovative drug and the arrival of its first competitor. Within one to three more years, the average decline in the leader's market share approached 50 percent (*Study to Assess Impacts of Releasing Safety and Effectiveness Data*, pp. 56, 58).

[32] Cocks, "Product Innovation," pp. 248–249.

implies that new data being incorporated into the summary differ from past data. The nature of competition in the industry suggests the ways in which the newer data will differ. Locally based firms in various countries could be expected to maintain control of established drugs that predate modern international competition. As these drugs are replaced by improvements from other sources,[33] the total local share will decline. The projected sales of a new drug in a given country will depend on the size of that country's market in the relevant therapeutic class, not alone on previous performance of the firm sponsoring the drug. Consequently, for projects in the development pipeline, the relative importance of different countries depends on the relative sizes of their drug markets and their consumers' receptiveness to new drugs.[34]

Table 3 shows the relative sizes of potential markets worldwide. Vulnerable new drug sales are recast in the form of percentages, indicating the maximum risk in foreign markets if a drug is introduced in the United States and data release induces foreign copies. The decision to market a drug in the United States must be made with a recognition of the impact on the sales *of that same drug* in other countries under consideration. Table 3 also distinguishes between patentable and unpatentable drugs, because the screen of patent protection cannot be considered of value for drugs that cannot meet statutory requirements of patentability in the United States or foreign countries.

The figures in Table 3 thus give an indication of the international demand for innovations and suggest consequences of a different nature. In introducing a new drug, the innovator may face a choice between the U.S. market and other markets likely to be lost to competition as a result of the release of data submitted to the FDA. Full disclosure of safety and efficacy data (the "twenty-foot reports") could risk 17.3 percent of total drug sales in the top nine foreign markets and 19.4 percent in the remainder. This compares with the 17.7 percent (and de-

---

[33] A recent example of a new drug that is replacing an older ulcer drug is SmithKline's anti-ulcer agent, Tagamet, that was introduced in sixty-five countries in 1977. SmithKline Corporation, *Annual Report*, 1978, p. 3.

[34] The inclination of foreign markets to adapt to new modes of therapy can significantly enhance the attractiveness of those therapies beyond the levels suggested by size alone. For example, total market revenue from new products introduced in Great Britain between 1968 and 1972 amounted to 90 percent of that generated by new products introduced in the United States, despite a market one-seventh the size. Revenue per drug in England was better than half that in the United States, even though some of the new drugs in England were competing among themselves, sharing markets. (Clymer, "Economic and Regulatory Climate," p. 147.)

TABLE 3
FOREIGN SALES OF PATENTABLE AND UNPATENTABLE DRUGS VULNERABLE TO DATA RELEASE, 1976

World Market for U.S. Pharmaceuticals	Total Pharmaceutical Sales[a]		Extent of Impact of S&E Release	% of Sales of Patentable Drugs[d] Vulnerable at Release of:			% of Sales of Unpatentable Drugs[d] Vulnerable at Release of:		
	Millions of dollars	Percent of world market		Individual case reports	Summary of case reports	Summary of clinical tests	Individual case reports	Summary of case reports	Summary of clinical tests
Japan	5,360	12.5	Minimal	0.0	0.0	0.0	0.0	0.0	0.0
West Germany	3,360	7.9	Possible	7.9	0.0	0.0	7.9	0.0	0.0
France	2,880	6.7	Minimal	0.0	0.0	0.0	0.0	0.0	0.0
Italy	2,000	4.7	Minimal	0.0	0.0	0.0	0.0	0.0	0.0
Spain	1,300	3.0	Possible	3.0	3.0	3.0	3.0	3.0	3.0
Brazil	1,200	2.8	Possible	2.8	2.8	2.8	2.8	2.8	2.8
United Kingdom	970	2.3	Minimal	0.0	0.0	0.0	2.3	0.0	0.0
Mexico	935	2.2	Possible	2.2	2.2	0.0	2.2	2.2	0.0
Canada	580	1.4	Probable	1.4	0.0	0.0	1.4	0.0	0.0
9 market total[b]	18,585	43.5		17.3	8.0	5.8	19.6	8.0	5.8
Other[c]	16,565	38.8		19.4	N/A	N/A	19.4	N/A	N/A
Foreign total[b]	35,150	82.3		36.7	8.0+	5.8+	39.0	8.0+	5.8+

a 1976 estimated data.　b Excludes United States.　c Includes about 150 other nations, including some third world countries.
d The patentability of drugs was evaluated separately for each foreign country, accounting for varying levels of patent protection accorded new drugs in each.
SOURCE: Authors' estimates based on information in FDA, "Supplemental Analysis of the Impact of Provision in S. 2755 Regarding Disclosure of Safety and Effectiveness Data on Foreign Markets of U.S. Multinational Firms," Tab C of enclosure to letter from the Director of FDA's Office of Legislative Services to members of Senate Subcommittee on Health and Scientific Resources and House Subcommittee on Health and Environment (June 16, 1978), Charts 1–3.

clining) market the United States has to offer (see Table 2).[35] For unpatentable drugs, the addition of the United Kingdom raises total foreign vulnerability in the top nine markets to 19.6 percent, compared with a domestic market that would be protected for five years only. To the extent that foreign markets, like Great Britain, respond to new drugs more readily than does the United States, these figures understate the impact of disclosure. Another factor mitigating the usefulness of the screens, which provided the number of countries likely to be affected, is that insufficiency of U.S. data to support a foreign drug application was considered adequate to protect a foreign market. To the extent that the U.S. data will reduce the cost (or obviate the necessity) of *some* foreign tests, the regulatory hurdle will be lowered and the risk of loss correspondingly raised.

That the United States will remain an important market for future phamaceuticals is obvious. Simple comparisons of the relative size of the U.S. market and the market placed at risk by disclosure policy will not reveal a critical point at which it is no longer profitable to market a drug in the United States. For important patentable therapeutic advances, the alternatives faced by the innovators will not be so bleak as the complete sacrifice of some markets for the sake of others. Instead, there will be sequential introductions of drugs in the different countries. Markets susceptible to a substantial risk of follow-on competition would be developed first in order to establish the new product. Submission of a monograph to the FDA could be delayed to reduce the impact of generic competition abroad. The impact in foreign markets need not approach the dimensions of the potential U.S. demand before these foreign markets become important factors in the timing of release in this country. If sales were jeopardized by monograph release, and the extent of this jeopardy could be reduced by first incorporating a drug into foreign health care systems, the cost of postponing U.S. introduction would amount only to a reduction in the present value of the drug's revenue stream, not the entire anticipated returns. Thus, if markets one-half the size of the U.S. market could be insulated by a two-year United

---

[35] In 1973, the U.S. share of the world pharmaceutical market stood at 20.3 percent, while the share of smaller foreign markets (excluding the top nine) was 34.1 percent. However, the slower growth in the U.S. (and the decline of the U.S. position), significant as it was, was not as important as the growth in the developing countries. Sales in these markets grew 78.5 percent in the three years, compared with a 46 percent growth for the ten top markets. It is in the less developed countries that the potential for further growth remains the highest, suggesting further erosion of the relative prominence of the United States and other major countries. Barrie James, *The Future of the Multinational Pharmaceutical Industry* (New York: The Halsted Press, 1977), p. 7.

States delay, the loss of perhaps 20 percent in the value of U.S. returns would clearly be justified by the foreign gains.[36]

How the decisions to market a drug are affected by disclosure will depend on several factors: foreign reactions to the change in disclosure policy in the United States, the rate of sales deterioration following the advent of generic competition, the expected commercial life of the product, the number of vulnerable markets, and their size relative to the U.S. market. With allowance for the size of the smaller foreign markets placed at risk (according to FDA's estimates) and the likely growth of these markets in the future, their size will assume increasing importance over time. Already these smaller foreign markets in total may have passed the U.S. market in size. Pracon's estimates of the deterioration of sales caused by follow-on competition[37] can be regarded as at least a minimum estimate of the impact generic equivalents would have on the leading firms. In those countries where drugs are purchased and distributed by a central authority, sales losses as a result of new competitive options could be sudden and severe.

The significant drugs (those which promise greater revenues, wider distribution, and longer drug life) would be likely to be subject to longer delays in U.S. marketing than the minor advances with limited market potential. For the major drugs, more foreign sales would be vulnerable, and they would remain vulnerable longer, while the demand-in-waiting in the United States would tend to subside less quickly than for minor ones. Introductions of less commercial importance would not afford great opportunity for selective marketing, and, because their commercial lives are more limited than those of major breakthroughs, the impact of United States data release would not contribute significantly to their demise abroad.

It is important to distinguish unpatentable entities from the drugs just discussed. Although unpatented drugs may be less important on the average than the typical patented product, the domestic consequences of a change in U.S. policy would probably be more pronounced. For

---

[36] This analysis tends to support the reactions reported by PMA that member firms would establish new drugs in foreign markets before seeking FDA approval. According to one firm, it would be preferable "to market a new drug in all other countries before the United States if we would have to comply with the new provisions . . . giving confidential information to all competitors in the world." The preference for foreign markets is corroborated by U.S. firms, which predict an accelerated transfer of research overseas. Statement of C. Joseph Stetler, President, PMA, in U.S. Congress, Health Subcommittee, Committee on Interstate and Foreign Commerce, House of Representatives, *Hearings on H.R. 11611*, 95th Congress, 2d session, pt. 2, June 15, 1978, pp. 1976–1983.

[37] See note 31.

unpatented drugs, the proposed legislation provides five-year protection from competition in the same market by prohibiting the use of released data in subsequent applications. As noted, current approval practices can substitute for patent protection, a fact that might be critical to the success of a drug without the formal legal recourse of a patent. If the regulatory processes overseas provide a longer life than the five years contemplated for the United States, the relative importance of the U.S. market will diminish accordingly. Especially in the cases of commercially important but unpatented drugs, limited revenues in the United States may not be worth the risk of disclosure of valuable data in the new drug process until foreign sales begin to fade by themselves.

Thus one can see unfolding a different picture of pharmaceutical innovations from the one revealed by the supply models postulated earlier. To be sure, to the extent that internal financing remains *the* viable method for undertaking such ventures, reduced profitability and diminished funds available for research will work a simultaneous effect on R&D investment. The supply effect is one working on the industry as a whole, an industry becoming increasingly (although by no means completely) insulated from the regulatory fluctuations in one element of its marketing portfolio. If a small country were to propose regulatory reform similar to that proposed here, it is not difficult to imagine the industry sacrificing that market entirely rather than risking substantial losses elsewhere. The relevant question in the formulation of U.S. policy is how much longer the United States can depend on the scope and wealth of its markets to outweigh the international interests of the pharmaceutical manufacturers.

Trade Secrets, Competitive Advantage, and Research Information

Until this point, all of the analysis and most of the debate on the issue of releasing safety and efficacy data has centered on the consequence of direct product competition for innovative drugs. Even the minimal estimates of impact translate into millions of dollars lost by the progressive pharmaceutical firms—a sum worth the effort to protect. The fact that the dollar impact in this area is relatively minor in comparison to the larger fund from which it would be drawn, however, has led reformers to discount the adverse consequences.

Largely ignored in the exchange have been industry arguments that the information has a value beyond the immediate purposes of obtaining subsequent approval for the same drug. Certainly a significant part of the value of data used in support of a new drug application comes from the fact that it advances a new product toward market and hoped-for profits. But the industry has cited other competitive advantages that would be lost through disclosure. "It is apparent that competitors could take advantage of the innovator's data, either in terms of developing a variation of his product which does not infringe on his patent or in terms of pursuing a quite different discovery."[38] Serendipitous observations and unexplored leads revealed in the testing process would be available to competitors. Moreover, the more innovative firms fear that the testing process itself, which may be more highly developed in certain firms, may be revealed, with a subsequent loss in the advantage the process confers.[39]

Claims regarding the commercial value of assets that firms themselves consider confidential are difficult to assess objectively. Possessors of trade secrets cannot demonstrate the value of the secrets without revealing and thereby destroying them. With only meager evidence, the debates on this issue have hinged on the credibility of the parties making the assertions. But if direct evidence is not available, perhaps one can find indirect evidence (suggested by economic inferences) to shed light on the problem.[40] Although the picture may not emerge clearly, the indirect evidence can nonetheless disclose patterns otherwise invisible.

If one cannot observe the transactions in which property in trade secrets is exchanged and thus appraise the value of the secrets, one may check for the use of resources to prevent disclosure: the very existence

---

[38] Stetler, Statement in *Hearings on 11611*, p. 1981.

[39] Similar claims have been made by pesticide manufacturers, who recently faced similar legislation and are now operating under it. Federal Insecticide, Fungicide and Rodenticide Act (FIFRA), section 3(c)(1)(D). See Statement of John E. Donalds, General Manager, Agricultural Products Department, Dow Chemical U.S.A., in U.S. Congress, House of Representatives, Committee on Agriculture, *Hearings, Federal Insecticide, Fungicide and Rodenticide Act*, 95th Congress, 1st session, pt. 3, March 9, 1977, pp. 310–336.

It is noteworthy that in FIFRA protection of information regarded by a company as a trade secret is provided explicitly. In the proposed measures regarding disclosure of drug information, however, protection of such information is specifically denied. The relevant section of the Food, Drug, and Cosmetic Act that protects trade secrets, 21 U.S.C., section 331(j), and the general criminal sanction against disclosure, 18 U.S.C., section 1905, are declared inapplicable. The only privilege preserved in the pending legislation is that of personal information, such as doctor-patient relations, as exempted in the Freedom of Information Act, 5 U.S.C., section 552(b)(6). Thus, there will be *no* privilege of confidentiality accorded to any of the commercial information revealed in the data subject to release.

[40] Direct evidence would be the existence of an established market in which the property in question is traded at a price. The price would indicate the value of the good. Unfortunately, the market for trade secrets is also itself secret; details of the transactions, if not the transactions themselves, are not made known to anyone but the transacting parties.

of elaborate legal systems and doctrines to protect research information suggests that it is valuable. Some evidence on this is provided in a recent judicial opinion involving requirements upon the pesticide industry to disclose technological data to the Environmental Protection Agency:

> Nor is it disputed that the information, research and test data developed by or for plaintiff and submitted by it is confidentially maintained by plaintiff. Except for efficiency data, this information is not disclosed generally except to the EPA and other governmental agencies pursuant to their regulatory requirements. Circulation of these reports among plaintiff's personnel is on a need-to-know basis and plaintiff's personnel execute security agreements with respect to this information, research, and test data.[41]

It is unlikely that the measures described here are directed entirely against the possibility that a competitor would be able to use the data for a subsequent application with the EPA. Data presented to a government agency as evidence on one issue may not, without adaptation or verification, serve a studious competitor's rival research interests. They can nevertheless be competitively advantageous in affording clues about what the innovative firm has done or is doing and thus about what research tracks may be taken.

The standard approach in modern-day pharmaceutical research is to formulate and test, systematically and exhaustively, new compounds analogous to known compounds with desired pharmaceutical properties. This is the process sometimes referred to pejoratively as "molecular manipulation." This research, like all pharmaceutical research, is costly. One can readily see that a rival's information relating to any compounds of interest, including identification of families of compounds of interest and negative results, may be valuable.[42] It happens in the pharmaceutical industry that companies will sometimes buy, as an entity, another's research effort, including formulas, procedures for synthesis, and results-to-date, rather than duplicating the work to create the data.

---

[41] Mobay Chemical Corp. v. Costle, 447 F.Supp. 811, 827 (W.D.Mo. 1978).

[42] Consider, for example, the post-World War II publication by American intelligence teams of the results of their investigation of German wartime research on synthetic analgesics and the effect of that publication in America, recounted in Eli Lilly & Co., Inc. v. Generic Drug Sales, Inc., 324 F.Supp. 715 (S.D.Fla. 1971), aff'd 460 F.2d 1096 (5th Cir. 1972). The lower court opinion includes an interesting account of the large-scale screening and testing of compounds, and of sponsorship by the National Academy of Science of a committee of experts to facilitate "annual meetings for exchange of research data among scientists working in the drug companies, universities, and other laboratories, and the U.S. Commissioner of Narcotics" (pp. 717–718).

Evidence on the quality of the research process is highly tentative. It is difficult to determine whether one method for testing drugs is better than another, even granting full knowledge of the two processes. As a result, we have chosen a proxy that may give some indication of the relative success of different firms in testing for safety and efficacy of their new products. By law, the ultimate judge of safety and efficacy data is the FDA. Test quality has been a factor in the regulatory delays cited by critics of the agency. From 1967 through 1969, in response to the complaints, the FDA released a breakdown of reasons for incomplete NDAs. The lists showed that, on average, 25 percent of the applications were unapprovable for lack of sufficient animal safety data, 59 percent were unapprovable because of insufficient clinical safety data, and 60 percent suffered from critically deficient clinical efficacy data.[43] Of course, the FDA's strict standards have been called into question, but that need not concern us here. Regardless of what the standards may have been since the passage of the 1962 amendments, one would expect the firms with relatively better development programs and testing procedures to experience fewer and shorter delays. That is, if some firms consistently obtain new drug approval more quickly than their competitors, an implication is that the speedier firms are those that have discovered improved methods of testing.

Table 4 gives the relative approval time for the eight leading companies for drugs in a sample of the most active therapeutic categories in the period 1963 to 1975. Included in these categories are the anti-infectives, cardiovasculars, diuretics, cancer chemotherapies, and others. Average approval time was normalized (set equal to a value of one) for each individual category and for each of three time periods, 1963–1965, 1966–1969, and 1970–1975, so that each drug's approval delay could be expressed as a departure from the average in its class. The data show that there is indeed a difference across firms in the relative time required for approval of a drug. Firms with short approval times were also those with extensive experience in applying for approval of new chemical entities. Generally, the more introductions a firm produced, the less time the FDA would take to approve its drugs. The average time for the least effective firm's applications was about twice the average time for the best.

To be sure, many factors enter into the time required for approval of an NDA: the relationship between the sponsoring firm and the agency, the scientific novelty of the drug, and the individual firm's policy in pursuing approval, to name just three. Thus, the evidence offered here

---

[43] Calculated from FDA annual reports, 1967–1968.

TABLE 4

SHARE OF NEW CHEMICAL ENTITIES APPROVED AND RELATIVE NDA
APPROVAL TIME IN MAJOR THERAPEUTIC CATEGORIES, LEADING
EIGHT FIRMS AND LEAST INNOVATIVE FIRMS, 1963–1975

Firm	Share of Entities[a] (percent)	Relative Approval Time and 95% Confidence Interval (Average Approval Time = 1.0)[b]
A	15	.93 ± .46
B	13	.66 ± .21
C&D[c]	11	.82 ± .24
E	8	.73 ± .52
F	6	1.12 ±1.26
G&H[c]	4	1.31 ± .22
Least active	2[d]	1.21 ± .26

[a] Based on sample of sixty-four total introductions.
[b] Approval time normalized for therapeutic category and date of introduction.
[c] Firms with equal number of introductions.
[d] Average share for eleven least active firms.
SOURCE: Product Coordination Staff, New Drug Evaluation, Bureau of Drugs, Food and Drug Administration.

must be considered cautiously. It does, however, indicate more than a random distribution of approval delays among firms. It seems to suggest that those firms that would be expected to have efficient testing programs do indeed have them. Consequently, there may be some validity to industry claims that the release of safety and efficacy data could reveal trade secrets about the process of research and development.

We now turn our attention to the disclosure rules of S.2755 in the context of the general policy of industrial property protection as developed by the patent system. First, let us review the way S.2755 would treat the disclosure of monograph data. In doing so, it is helpful to compare the proposed S.2755 procedures with those for obtaining a patent in the United States. The comparison can be made according to the amount and kinds of data required and the submitter's control over the data once submitted. The bill would require a petitioner for a monograph on a new pharmaceutical compound to file more extensive data than are required from an inventor in submitting an application for a patent on the compound (just as the FDA does now). The data disclosed in the patent application are currently printed as part of the patent document, and, to the extent not covered by the claims of that or another patent, pass into the public domain upon issuance.[44]

The existing patent statute does not require patent applicants to make full disclosure of research or clinical data. They must, as a condition of receiving their patents, present a "written description of the invention, and of the manner and process of making or using it, in such full, clear, concise and exact terms as to enable any person skilled in the art to which it pertains . . . to make and use same. . . ."[45] The statute also requires that the applicant "shall set forth the best mode contemplated by the inventor of carrying out his invention."[46] The statute does not required that applicants disclose every mode of practicing (making use of) their inventions or the know-how or special data useful but not indispensable to practicing those inventions. Instead, the statute allows applicants to elect between federal patent protection or common law trade secret protection, sets the minimal disclosure standards necessary to satisfy a patent application, and allows the inventors to husband the balance of their data, if they like, as trade secrets.

The patent application for a new drug is normally filed as soon as animal experimentation establishes proof of a desired pharmacological property. The application for FDA approval of an IND and subsequent NDA follows. In the period subsequent to filing patent applications, applicants typically extend their research, particularly in animal and clinical testing and in developing manufacturing procedures. Normally, the data from this extended research are intended to support the INDs and the NDAs. Both the resulting data and the techniques of acquiring them can, under traditional principles, constitute trade secrets, and may yield additional patentable inventions. The new data are new property. And with the creation of the new data, the owner-creator of the data is presented with a fresh choice between the alternate modes of patent or

---

[44] Rip Van Winkles Bed Co. v. Murphy Wall Bed Co., 1 F.2d 673, 679 (9th Cir. 1924); Anthony Deller, *Deller's Walker on Patents*, section 242, 2d ed. (Mount Kisco, N.Y.: Baker, Voorhis & Co., Inc., 1965).

[45] 35 U.S.C., section 112.

[46] Ibid. The courts are breathing fresh life into the best mode requirement, but there has not yet been any departure from the rule that a patent applicant must disclose the best mode "contemplated" by the inventor at the time the application is filed. Dugald McDougall, "The Courts Are Telling Us: 'Your Client's Best Mode Must Be Disclosed,'" *Journal of the Patent Office Society*, vol. 59 (1977), pp. 321 ff. The applicant is not required to disclose a "mode" superior to that disclosed in the application if found subsequent to the application. See, however, J. Philip Anderegg, "The Best Mode Requirement of 35 U.S.C. 112," *American Patent Law Association Quarterly*, vol. 6 (1978), pp. 219 ff.

trade-secret protection.[47] The two modes of protection of industrial property differ in terms and conditions of exclusivity; both provide commercial advantage over rivals.

The provisions of S.2755 would limit the value of the data developed by the innovator and required as a part of the application for a monograph but extending beyond that required in a patent application —that is, material that would normally be considered proprietary. Under the new legislation, manufacturing, marketing, and financial data would continue to be protected, but all the animal and clinical testing data would be disclosed, before the monograph hearing, to members of the public who satisfy the agency that they are not likely to use it for commercial purposes. After approval of the monograph, disclosure would be made to the public at large, including commercial rivals.

These data can include the protocols or instrumentation used in the tests. To a sophisticated entrepreneur, they would provide clues to alternate pharmacological uses of the compound in the application or to the properties (or experimental possibilities) of related compounds or to confirmation (or disproof) of a rival firm's experimental strategies or hypotheses. The hazards of improper or inadvertent disclosure to rival interests in the prehearing period are obvious.

One need not assume that a rival, gleaning such information from the file, must immediately put the information to commercial use in order for the innovator to be injured competitively. In research, time is a crucial advantage, whether in preparing for commercial market entry or in the course of patent protection. The value of that time is acknowledged for trade secrets in judicial decisions in which the value of the injury from trade secret misappropriation is measured by the value of time gained.[48]

Considering only the advantage to a follower in shortening his time to market entry (within the five-year post-license period), we note that the follower may simply replicate the file data and avoid false starts and trial-and-error adjustments with experimental strategies. After the five years, the follower may, riding on the innovator's data, obtain a license on a minimal and comparatively inexpensive showing of pharmacological properties.

---

[47] The inventor must retain the right to elect the data disclosed in a patent application beyond the point where the Patent Office has allowed claims and the applicant knows what the scope of protection will be. Patent applications are kept in secrecy (35 U.S.C., section 122). Abandoned applications are not open to public inspection except in limited circumstances (37 CFR, section 1.14(b)).

[48] For example, Winston Research Corp. v. Minnesota Mining & Mfg. Co., 350 F.2d 134 (9th Cir. 1965).

The five-year protection period of section 121, S.2755, will govern market entry in the United States but not abroad. Competitors will be free to use the innovator-applicant's own data, within that five-year period, in the foreign markets. These markets, as this paper has already shown, are of increasing importance. This point, once stated, needs no elaboration.

Whatever the outer limits of the changes that the proposed procedures will work in the choices available to applicants, the hazard of disclosure of proprietary information will be increased, and the cost of that hazard will necessarily be reckoned into research decisions and allocations.

More important, after the five-year exclusive period, the data contained in the monograph will be fully available to competitors. Because of the comprehensive nature of those data, much competitively valuable information will be disclosed. Under the current system of protecting industrial property, pharmaceutical firms have the option of treating this information as trade secrets. Whether intentionally or not, S.2755 would significantly alter chances of preserving the exclusivity and confidentiality of information created in invention and innovation.

The importance of trade secrets was recently reaffirmed by the Supreme Court.[49] In a case broadly challenging the protectability of such secrets, the Court noted that "trade secret law will encourage invention in areas where patent law does not reach, and will permit the independent innovator to proceed with the discovery and exploitation of his invention. Competition is fostered and the public is not deprived of the use of a valuable, if not quite patentable, invention."[50]

To entrepreneurs, both trade secrecy and patents are indispensable components of the entire set of industrial property rights. The importance of trade secrets was recently expressed in the following manner by former U.S. Commissioner of Patents Edward J. Brenner in his amicus brief in the Chrysler case before the Supreme Court on behalf of the Association for the Advancement of Invention and Innovation:

> Often, the key to a successful commercialization effort may lie in what superficially appears to be an insignificant or obscure piece of information. Such bits and fragments of information often have proved to be the "missing link" between conception and successful development or marketing of an idea. Businesses (and individuals) as a matter of ordinary practice seek to obtain and analyze all of the information

---

[49] Kewanee Oil Corp. v. Bicron Corp., 416 U.S. 470 (1974).
[50] Ibid., p. 485.

which they can acquire concerning related plans and activities of their competitors. This kind of information can very materially aid a competitor to piece together the existence, nature, and objectives of a project which may heavily involve inventions and innovations.[51]

For these reasons, S.2755 will affect adversely the value of trade secrets or confidential data submitted by applicants for monographs to the FDA. The reduction in value will necessarily be figured as a cost in the cost-benefit analysis of research and development.

Conclusions

In section 101 of S.2755, the Congress finds it to be in the "interest of the American people to encourage . . . the increase of knowledge regarding disease . . . and the discovery and development of safe and effective drug products. . . ." In this paper, we have investigated the economics of pharmaceutical information in the context of the proposed regulatory reforms. Because the use of information is worldwide and because pharmaceutical production can freely move across borders, we have focused our analysis on the international implications of the proposed reforms. Our analysis is in agreement with those studies that indicate a reduction in total research and development effort as a consequence of the current proposed regulations in S.2755. We further suggest that the impact on the U.S. operations of the industry will be disproportionate.

Equally important, preliminary evidence indicates that there are distinct comparative advantages in the production and use of information. Our analysis also concludes that the provisions of S.2755 that will reveal information surrounding those processes may seriously reduce returns from further developing these skills. In its present form, S.2755 also significantly alters the traditional rights to industrial property for firms operating within the United States. Specifically, it undesirably curtails the range of choices by inventors and entrepreneurs between trade secrets or patent protection, and much of the information traditionally protected as trade secrets would no longer be protected.[52]

---

[51] Edward J. Brenner in *Brief Amicus Curiae*, Chrysler Corp. v. Brown, 441 U.S. 281 (1979); reprinted in *Action* (May/June 1978), p. 5. See also, Exxon Corp. v. F.T.C. 589 F.2d 582.

[52] The Federal Insecticide, Fungicide and Rodenticide Act (7 U.S.C., secs. 135–136) gives explicit protection to industrial property disclosed in regulatory procedures formerly protected by trade secret law.

Commentary

Daniel K. Benjamin

The common questions that tie together the papers by Kitch and by Clarkson, Ladd, and MacLeod are fundamental and controversial: How does the appropriability of the returns from pharmaceutical innovation affect the amount of such innovation? To what extent have existing FDA regulations affected this appropriability, and is it likely to be affected by proposed changes in the regulations? Satisfactory answers to these questions would yield a significant improvement in our understanding of the innovative process in all lines of activity. Yet, because so many things besides FDA behavior affect the returns from pharmaceutical innovation, agreement on the validity of a given set of answers is costly to achieve.

Kitch's paper is based largely on the important work he recently published in the *Journal of Law and Economics*.[1] In the course of that work, Kitch tabulated fifty important inventions, their dates of patentability and their dates of commercial introduction. The average delay between patentability and introduction for those fifty inventions was 28.7 years. There are, of course, some extremes in Kitch's sample: 83 years elapsed between the patentability of the fluorescent light and its commercial introduction, while the delay was 153 years for the jet engine. To reduce the effect of these extremes, I arbitrarily eliminated from the list every item for which there was a delay of more than fifty years. For the truncated list, the average delay between patentability and commercial feasibility was exactly 17 years, which suggests that either Kitch's sample is not random or that the patent system has little effect.

ACKNOWLEDGMENT: Discussions with Levis Kochin have improved the quality of this comment, without (to my knowledge) introducing any additional errors.

[1] Edmund W. Kitch, "The Nature and Function of the Patent System," *Journal of Law and Economics*, vol. 20, no. 2 (October 1977), pp. 265–280. I highly recommend this paper to anyone who has an interest in patents. See also his article in this volume, "The Political Economy of Innovation in Drugs and the Proposed Drug Regulation Reform Act of 1978."

116

The point of this exercise is twofold. First, much has been written about the short effective life of pharmaceutical patents and the deleterious effects thereof on pharmaceutical innovation. Presumably, those who have commented on this issue have meant to imply that the effective patent life for pharmaceuticals is shorter than for other inventions and the adverse effects on innovation thus greater. Yet Kitch's work suggests that substantial delays between patentability and commercial introduction are not uncommon, and I know of no one who has ascertained whether those delays are any greater for pharmaceuticals than for anything else.

Perhaps more germane to our inquiry is the extent to which the regulatory process has lengthened the delay between the patentability of drugs and their commercial introduction. Ronald Hansen's work indicates that it now takes six to seven years for an NCE to complete the regulatory process.[2] In order to illustrate the effect of this on expected returns, I assume for simplicity that the profits from a new drug are level throughout the effective patent life and drop to zero when the patent expires.[3] At a discount rate of 10 percent, eliminating only the first five years of the profit stream reduces the present value of profits by 50 percent; eliminating the first seven years reduces the present value by 60 percent. At a 20 percent discount rate, the reductions in present values are 62 percent and 75 percent, respectively. Inasmuch as U.S. regulations truncate effective patent lives only in the United States, it is necessary to take into account that only a portion of the profits from a new drug come from U.S. sales. Using U.S. new drug sales as a percentage of worldwide new drug sales as a crude measure of the importance of U.S. profits, I will assume that one half of the total profits from new drug sales would come from the United States in the absence of our more stringent regulations. The implied reduction in worldwide profitability of innovation due to U.S. regulations is thus 25 percent to 30 percent at a discount rate of 10 percent, and 30 percent to 38 percent at a rate of 20 percent.

In order to assess the effects of this decline in profitability on the rate of innovation, one must have some notion of the way in which

---

[2] Ronald W. Hansen, Testimony before FDA Commissioner Donald M. Kennedy, September 29, 1977. Also published in abbreviated form as, *Comments on the Proposed Change in the FDA's Trade Secrets Policy*, PS7706 (Rochester: The Center for the Study of Drug Development, University of Rochester, October 1977).

[3] The assumption of a level profits stream certainly overestimates the effects on some drugs and underestimates the effects on others. The essential point is that *delay* is socially costly.

both the demand and the supply of innovation respond to the returns thereof. In order to continue to minimize my computational efforts, I shall simply assume that both the demand and supply of innovation are unit-elastic.[4] Under this assumption, a 25 percent reduction in expected profitability as a result of regulatory delays implies a 14 percent decline in innovation; a 38 percent reduction in profitability implies a 21 percent decline in innovation.

Although I am unaware that anyone has done these calculations, the general idea behind them is nothing new. Indeed, the recognition of the effects of regulatory delay on innovation has been the source of proposals to restore the effective patent life on pharmaceuticals to its pre-1962 levels. One method of doing this would be to have the Patent Office restart the clock on a drug's patent in the event it successfully completed the NDA process. Such a solution, however, is little more than a palliative. Consider, for example, the case of a five-year regulatory delay with a discount rate of 10 percent. Restoring the effective patent life to seventeen years by adding five years onto the future end of the patent would restore only about one-fifth the loss in profitability caused by the regulatory delay. Indeed, there is no extension of patent life capable of fully offsetting a five-year delay. Even if drug patents were granted in perpetuity, the present value of profits would still be 20 percent lower than in the preregulatory climate. This is not to say that attempts to extend the effective patent life for drugs are pointless, only that plausible extensions will not have a major impact on profitability or on innovation.

Kitch goes on to argue that, without effective patent protection, negative or mundane results would not be communicated among pharmaceutical researchers. If this is the case, then it seems to me that drug research is unlike any other of which I am aware.[5] In economics— and colleagues in engineering and physics tell me the same story— ostensibly only the positive results get published. However, by looking at the structure of someone's theoretical model or the structure of his empirical work one can immediately, or at least far faster than whoever originally did the work, see what dead ends the author must have run into and what the dead ends of further research on the topic are likely to be. Insofar as mundane results are concerned, I would only note that the plethora of second- and third-rate journals suggests that there is a

---

[4] That is, a given percentage decline in the returns from innovation will yield an equal percentage decline in the quantity of innovation supplied.

[5] Except perhaps in law. One finds it difficult to imagine a lawyer announcing to a judge, "Well, here are the crummy things about our case."

118

market for these results as well. To be sure, the rewards for publishing mundane results are lower than for publishing wildly exciting results, but then so too are the social benefits those results yield.

The principal area of overlap between the papers by Kitch and by Clarkson, Ladd, and MacLeod concerns proposals to require the FDA to release all of the information contained in an NDA at some time (perhaps immediately) after a drug is approved for marketing. The authors of both papers argue that the forced disclosure of this information will unambiguously reduce the amount of pharmaceutical innovation. On a priori grounds, however, I think the effect of disclosure on innovation is ambiguous.

Consider first a setting in which the industry is highly competitive, and suppose that it is cheap for firms to exchange information through publishing or cross-licensing or simply by selling the information outright. In such a setting, the act of innovation produces both a drug and a body of information, each of which can be sold. If the firm is forced to disclose information without compensation, then the returns from innovation, and hence the amount of innovation, will fall. Moreover, there will not be any offsetting additional innovation by other firms, because they would already have obtained all of the useful information through exchange.

At the other end of the spectrum is what might be called a Nader model. Suppose that innovation currently occurs randomly and at no expense and that it is prohibitively costly for firms to capture the value of the information they possess through exchanges with other firms. In this case, disclosure will not reduce innovation by the original group of firms (because the innovation is by assumption a random process outside of their control), but it will yield an increase in innovation by the other firms who use the information that is now available. Thus, the net effect will be to increase innovation.

Anywhere between these two cases there will be a mixture of the two forces at work. On the one hand, the loss of part of the property rights associated with innovation will tend to reduce innovative activity; on the other, the wider dissemination of any given stock of knowledge will tend to increase innovation. My view is that the world is much closer to the first model than to the second. The important point, however, is that the parties to the debate over disclosure should be aware of the structures they (and their opponents) are implicitly imposing on the world.

There is a second issue here that is recognized by neither of the two papers. It is my impression that there are some drugs for which it

119

is very easy to develop substitutes—all one needs is a quick look at the active molecule. For these drugs, the potential benefits of disclosure are small and so too are the potential effects of disclosure. Whether or not there is disclosure, such drugs will quickly face wholesale competition. There are other drugs, however, that are extremely resistant to competitive innovation, without the detailed information that would be revealed by disclosure. For these drugs, U.S. consumers will be put in an all-or-nothing position. If a firm introduces such a drug into the U.S. market, it can obtain additional profits on its U.S. sales, but its foreign profits will be reduced by competitive innovation brought on by disclosure. If the potential U.S. profits exceed the loss in foreign profits, the firm will enter the U.S. market; if this inequality is reversed, it will not. Thus for this type of drug, a disclosure requirement increases the risk faced by U.S. consumers. Moreover, the U.S. market has been a shrinking share of the total market for pharmaceuticals; if this trend continues, it becomes increasingly likely that the net effects of disclosure will be negative for U.S. consumers.

It is to the credit of Clarkson and his coauthors that they go beyond their theoretical analysis with an attempt to estimate the effects of disclosure on research and development activity. To do so, they use a model in which a firm's sales determine its R&D expenditures. As they admit, such a model is not generally consistent with wealth maximization. The justification they offer for their approach is that, as an empirical matter, sales and R&D are closely correlated. I find this justification troubling on two grounds. First, work by Douglas Cocks implies that it is (successful) R&D expenditures that determine sales, not the other way around.[6] Second, any observed correlation between sales and R&D expenditures is presumably the outcome of an underlying constrained maximization problem. The observed empirical regularity will be useful in predicting the future only if the constraints facing firms do not change in an observationally relevant manner. I do not think this condition is satisfied in the case at hand. Forced disclosure of safety and efficacy data would represent a fundamental change in the proprietary rights to innovation. Any approach that assumes that this will have no effect on a firm's R&D-to-sales ratio should be viewed with great circumspection.

The most ingenious aspect of the Clarkson, Ladd, and MacLeod paper is the attempt to bring indirect evidence to bear on the disclosure

---

[6] Douglas L. Cocks, "Product Innovation and the Dynamic Elements of Competition in the Ethical Pharmaceutical Industry," in Robert B. Helms, ed., *Drug Development and Marketing* (Washington: American Enterprise Institute, 1975), p. 254.

debate. One element of the innovative process (under present regulations) is the ability to convince the FDA quickly and cheaply of a drug's safety and efficacy. The existence of substantial differences in approval times achieved by different companies would suggest that the speedier firms possess valuable information regarding the regulatory process—information that might be revealed by a disclosure requirement. Clarkson and his coauthors present evidence suggesting that there are in fact such differences among firms, in particular that firms with more experience in dealing with the FDA are able to obtain faster approval for their drugs. Based on the summary data presented, I was able to perform a Chi-square test of their hypothesis. The results indicate that there is an 80 percent chance that the observed inverse relationship between regulatory experience and regulatory delay is due to chance. Even if the three most experienced firms are compared to the rest, there is still a 20 percent chance that the observed relationship is due to chance. In short, although I am sympathetic with the approach, I am unconvinced by the results.

Fay H. Dworkin

I will confine my comments to those aspects of the papers that deal with specific implications of the proposed bill to revise the drug approval process.[1] I do this not only because it is a topic I know something about, but also because it is one of few threads common to both papers. But first I ought to issue a warning that my friends believe I was born a skeptic—I generally have a "show me" attitude. Many of the contentions these papers make are provocative, but they can be persuasive only if they are first cast in the form of hypotheses and then put to empirical test. None of this can be done, of course, without some grounding in theory.

Let us begin by taking a brief look at the findings of the papers on the proposed bill. Professor Kitch claims that the FDA is an inefficient manager of the scarce resources of drug research. I take this to mean that regulatory reform should begin by returning to the drug firms the power to allocate resources. Instead, the bill's "research-forcing" authority allows the FDA to redirect scientific resources, allocating them to studies of new uses for marketed drugs or other postmarketing investigations—which presumably forces research away from innova-

---

[1] U.S., Congress, House of Representatives, *The Drug Regulation Reform Act of 1978*, Pub. J.29–001–B5, 95th Cong., 2d sess., 1978, H.R. 11611. Also introduced in the Senate as S. 2755.

tive activity. Regarding the bill's provisions for subsidies to drug research, Kitch remarks that there will be no net increase in direct innovative activity unless the funds support work that would not otherwise have been done. Moreover, government subsidies offer no incentives for those carrying out the research to communicate their findings, because the recipients of public funds for research cannot obtain and exploit any patents resulting from their work. Finally, the bill's provision that confers a five-year period of exclusivity on safety and efficacy data is a further deterrent to research efficiency because it encourages duplicative research.

Kitch approaches the "supply of medicines" issue by searching for ways to optimize the efficiency of the research process. Thus, he finds that control of the timing and allocation of resources should reside in the R&D sector, which in turn should maintain open lines of communication to avoid duplication of effort. Patent systems come closer to achieving this desirable state than other solutions. In general, in his view, a patent system is superior to a trade-secrecy system because it allows the innovator to exercise control over the allocation of research resources, acts as a deterrent to duplication of effort, and encourages transactions among competitors by eliminating the fear of copying. It follows, then, that another reason the bill is deficient is that it does not lengthen the effective life of a patent.

Kitch bases his conclusions on an analysis of the impact of selected features of the bill on research efficiency. In my view, his failure to analyze other features of the bill (which also affect the research process) provides an unbalanced and unfair picture.

The bill would give the FDA the authority to order postmarketing investigations. Not only do we not know the extent to which this authority will be invoked, but we cannot judge whether such investigations will assume a large or small part of resources currently devoted to R&D. The bill would also give the FDA the authority to require that such studies be performed *jointly* by all the sponsors of the drug in question. To begin to assess the relative impact of this provision, we need to estimate the costs of various levels of postmarketing investigations. If, in fact, the future postmarketing investigations merely replace studies heretofore performed prior to approval, little change in research allocation will occur.

The thesis that research subsidies act to discourage the communication of negative findings can also be put to test. A search of the literature for reports on drugs under investigation can aid in comparing the extent to which the findings of private or public research are

122

published. Then we can compare the incidence of "positive" and "negative" results published.

Does the bill's provision to protect safety and efficacy data for five years after monograph approval act to promote duplicative testing, as Kitch asserts? If I needed a ladder, and my neighbor had one that would be available to me but only after a week had passed, I would look first to the possibility of buying my own. However, if for some reason that ladder was deliverable only after six days' delay, I would consider the relative cost of the ladder compared to the cost of waiting an additional day. I think the five-year exclusivity provision is analogous to that situation, and I would recommend we determine the costs of duplicating data that in time would come "free" (making sure that I included as a cost factor the time required to generate independent data).

The bill has at least two other provisions, not mentioned by Kitch, that are relevant to the question of research efficiency. I call these to attention because Kitch's failure is obviously (from what has just been said) an unintentional oversight. One of these is the provision to reduce control on the innovative (or early) phases of clinical investigations. The bill restricts regulatory review of the early clinical phase of drug development to making sure human subjects are protected and leaves the scientific and other technical aspects of these early clinical studies in the hands of the drug sponsor. The other provision expedites the marketing of breakthrough drugs by permitting the issuance of a provisional monograph. This will permit accelerated approval, on a provisional basis, for certain drugs that offer a major therapeutic advantage.

Kitch states no position on the safety and efficacy data disclosure provision of the bill. We might be led to believe that he endorses the disclosure provision because he opposes the one feature of the bill that specifically mitigates the effects of disclosure, namely the five-year period of exclusivity. However, his opposition to the five-year grace period is that it does not effectively protect the innovator from encroachment because the term of protection is too short and because "the most important piece of information for a firm choosing research projects is often the knowledge that something can be done." Nevertheless, because Kitch suggested in 1972 that the "regulatory information in the NDA be made publicly available," we are led to believe that it is not disclosure that is at issue, but rather whether the NDA confers exclusivity in the form of a secondary patent for five, ten, or more years.

Let us turn now to Clarkson's view of the recent regulatory reform initiative. Clarkson focuses on one aspect of the bill: its provision for disclosure of safety and efficacy data. These data, submitted on behalf of an application for approval to market a drug in the United States, are now accorded "trade-secret" status; that is, the data are treated as proprietary. The "trade-secrets" policy confers a necessary competitive advantage, says Clarkson, insulating the innovator from competition. Moreover, safety and efficacy data disclosure may promote a type of patent infringement by revealing the "missing link" to development of close substitutes.

Clarkson's analysis, in centering on a "trade-secrets" issue, looks at the "supply of medicines" from the perspective of maintaining incentives to continued investment in R&D. Data disclosure risks market-share attrition, particularly on the international market. And the paper impresses upon us that we need to inquire into the dynamics of the future operations of the pharmaceutical industry and give particular attention to the corresponding sales patterns worldwide. Preliminary evidence, we are told, runs counter to some of the assumptions of the FDA's previous studies.

It has been said that "innovation effectively sows the seeds of its own destruction."[2] The better one's innovation, the more competition it stimulates. In self-defense, perhaps, the innovator is at least as active as his competitors in searching for improvements. In short, an industry whose lifeblood is innovation is likely to have developed a wide range of adaptive mechanisms both to forces within—its competitors—and to outside influences—regulation. Clarkson says some firms are apparently better than others at adapting to regulatory constraints. Approval times, we are told, vary markedly depending on the firm. There are other adaptive forces about which we still know very little. These may be worth searching for.

Clarkson discusses two related trends typically alleged to be out-growths of drug regulation; I suggest they may have other antecedents. These relate to the "where" and "when" of marketing a new drug. We have seen that there has been an increase in expenditures for foreign R&D and that the United States is not the country of introduction of all new drugs. I recognize it may be difficult to ascertain the reasons behind the decisions on where and when to market a new drug, because these strategies can fall under the "trade-secrets" rubric. Nevertheless, in addition to the differences in drug regulation from country to country, we can and should explore differences in patent laws and

---

[2] Barrie G. James, *The Future of the Multinational Pharmaceutical Industry to 1990* (New York: Halsted Press, 1977), p. 167.

patent life, differences in tax laws, and differences in "regulatory" climate regarding clinical investigations. Most important, we should account for the fact that morbidity patterns vary, even among developed nations, and the markets for drugs in certain therapeutic categories will vary accordingly.

The Clarkson paper raises several issues regarding the "value" of safety and efficacy data. There are a variety of ways we could define this value. The simplest would be by the cost of generating them. Nothing said today would encourage us to adopt that view, but I think we would agree that the data are worth at least as much as they cost to generate. One estimate, based on Clymer,[3] is about $2–4 million per drug over a period of three to five years.[4] I think the compelling reason we should explore the costs of generating safety and efficacy data is that these costs, multiplied by the number of repetitions, are a measure of the wasteful efforts of duplicative research.

The Clarkson paper sees additional value in safety and efficacy data. Hidden in the data (and it must be somewhat obscure if we are to believe the innovator failed to spot it) may be a clue to an improved therapeutic agent. This better drug, once developed and marketed, would then capture a share of the market held by the innovator. It is interesting that drug firms, who hold that their own safety and efficacy data are so valuable, do not regard the data produced by others to be equally valuable. I have come to believe that the "missing-link" theory is a hypothetical problem. Safety and efficacy data, for a single drug, are literally voluminous. Obscure clues to product improvement may be analogous to the proverbial needle-in-a-haystack. Are resources really worth expending for so highly improbable a payoff?

Nevertheless, the "missing-link" hypothesis can be tested. We can compare, for a specific sample of drugs in a therapeutic category, the time it takes an innovator to market a product that competes with an innovative chemical with the time it takes for a competitor to do the same thing. We would then be better able to assess the incremental value of full knowledge of the data.

Clarkson cites indirect evidence of the value of safety and efficacy data in the variability of approval times from one firm to another. The implication here is that a drug firm may be exceptionally proficient at executing clinical investigations (for example, in selection of number of

---

[3] H. A. Clymer, "The Economics of Drug Innovation," in M. Pernarowski and M. Darrach, eds., *The Development and Control of New Drug Products* (Vancouver, B.C.: Evergreen Press, 1971), p. 112.

[4] Clymer data updated to 1977.

subjects and duration of testing). The degree to which efficient execution of clinical studies derives from planning and management skills, not reported in the NDA and consequently not disclosed, is unknown. Still more evidence of the value of the data is attributed to the extent to which firms guard against disclosure. I think we need to look at the other side of the coin, too: To what degree are data voluntarily disclosed through publication in scientific journals? We know this occurs, but we do not know to what extent.

To summarize, the Drug Regulation Reform Act has stimulated much discussion and can lead us into new insights on regulation and innovation. The Kitch and Clarkson papers illustrate that serious reflection can produce testable hypotheses, but we should not stop here. I repeat my earlier plea for creative empiricism.

Francis J. Blee

In any analysis of pharmaceutical innovation, it is important to distinguish a unique risk associated with pharmaceutical research—the risk of research that by definition seeks to obtain new chemical substances ultimately to be ingested by humans. These potent chemical agents are in almost all cases, also by definition, potentially dangerous to the human body. Because each person is unique, the danger of side effects can arise in any stage of the research process; indeed, even after long and careful testing, serious side effects may emerge in the post-NDA marketing phase. The development of a serious side effect in a pharmaceutical innovation can virtually destroy the commercial value of the product and the economic value of the arduous research conducted over many years. In this sense, the risks associated with pharmaceutical research are unique. A defective computer can be corrected, a faulty automobile can be recalled, but a new pharmaceutical product that produces serious side effects virtually ceases to have a viable economic potential.

As Kitch predicted in a paper written in 1972,[1] the effect of delays in the marketing of new drugs would be, in effect, to shorten the patent term. The Center for the Study of Drug Development undertook a detailed analysis of new chemical entities introduced in the U.S. market between 1966 and 1977. Table 1 summarizes this study's finding that the effective patent life of these chemicals after NDA approval had

---

[1] Edmund W. Kitch, "The Patent System and the New Drug Application: An Evaluation of the Incentives for Private Investment in New Drug Research and Marketing," in Richard L. Landau, ed., *Regulating New Drugs* (Chicago: University of Chicago Press, 1973), pp. 81–107.

TABLE 1

Summary of Patent Clearance Times

Year of Introduction	Average Elapsed Time From IND Submission to NDA Approval (months)	Average Effective Life of Patent (years)
1966	34	13
1967	46	15
1968	55	13
1969	58	15
1970	59	13
1971	54	13
1972	57	13
1973	65	12
1974	60	12
1975	96	10
1976	78	12
1977	96	9
10-year average (1966–75)	58.4	12.9
11-year average (1966–76)	60.2	12.8
12-year average (1966–77)	63.2	12.5

Source: The Center for the Study of Drug Development, University of Rochester Medical Center.

fallen to ten to twelve years by 1976–1977 from a thirteen-to-fifteen-year average in the 1966–1969 period.[2]

It should be recognized that under the administration's proposed bill the period for approval of a new drug application would be extended to 360 days from the present 180. The industry believes that the proposed investigational new drug system will produce additional delays in the innovative phase of drug discovery.[3] Moreover, the administration proposes to shorten exclusivity of NDA data to a five-year period

[2] Unpublished data available from the Center for the Study of Drug Development, University of Rochester School of Medicine. An earlier version of this data is contained in testimony by Ronald W. Hansen before FDA Commissioner Donald W. Kennedy, September 29, 1977.

[3] For additional industry reaction, see Robert L. Dean, "How the Drug Act Adds Disincentives to the Search for New Drugs," *New England Journal of Medicine*, vol. 299 (August 24, 1978), pp. 413–415.

TABLE 2

R&D COST PER NEW CHEMICAL ENTITY

R&D Investment		New Chemical Entities		
Period of investment	Total amount (millions of dollars)	Period of introduction	Total number	Cost per New Entity (millions of dollars)
1957–61	917	1962–66	78	11.8
1962–66	1,486	1967–71	63	23.6
1967–71	2,562	1972–76	67	38.2

SOURCE: PMA Human Ethical Research Expenditures.

and then is likely to encourage the testing of patents by competitors eager to enter an attractive field, with no research investment.

An area of great concern is the proposed monograph system, which would encourage imitators to go to the courts to challenge the patent position of the innovator. The unfortunate effect of the proposed new regulations, then, would be to raise the regulatory barriers for innovators and lower them for imitators. If the approval process were to be lengthened, as proposed in the administration's bill, effective patent life would be shortened beyond the estimates made by the Center for the Study of Drug Development. This increased regulation would further emphasize Kitch's point that "the ability of a firm to control the timing of its research and marketing has been handed over to the FDA where the operation of regulatory resource constraints and uniform procedures caused delays unrelated to drug-specific cost-benefit relationships."

An internal analysis we have conducted on economic trends in the pharmaceutical industry adds support to the conclusions reached by Kitch and by Clarkson, MacLeod, and Ladd. As Table 2 indicates, during the fifteen-year period, 1962 through 1976, assuming a five-year lag between R&D investment and the introduction of a new chemical entity, the five-year average cost of a new product for the pharmaceutical industry rose from $12 million to $38 million. Hansen estimates the cost increased to $55 million by 1976.[4]

We have also developed a model for calculating the discounted

---

[4] Ronald W. Hansen, *The Pharmaceutical Development Process: Estimates of Current Development Costs and Times and the Effects of Regulatory Changes*. (Rochester: Center for Research in Government Policy, University of Rochester, August 1977), p. 51.

return on incremental investment for both the United States and worldwide pharmaceutical markets during the same fifteen-year period. For R&D investment, we used PMA expenditures for human ethical R&D from 1957 through 1971, which we broke into three five-year periods. Plant and equipment expenditures, based on industry averages for the three periods (24 to 28 percent of sales), were also introduced to provide an estimate of total investment. Again under the assumption that there was a five-year lag in introduction, a profit stream was estimated by taking sales for the new chemical entities introduced during the period from 1962 through 1976. We then estimated an average yearly sales figure for each product and applied a profit margin range of 12 to 25 percent before a deduction for R&D. Each product was given a fifteen-year commercial life, with sales projected at an average level for fifteen years. An allowance was made for working capital at 25 percent of sales. The results, shown in Table 3, indicate that for a 15 percent profit margin the discounted return on investment in the U.S. market ranged from 5.9 percent to negative for this fifteen-year period. The negative returns for the U.S. market indicate that the industry did not even recoup initial investment.

Table 3 also shows results for the worldwide market. In order to develop a worldwide market potential, U.S. sales were increased by 50 percent in the first sales period 1962–1966; for 1967–1971, we assumed international sales were 100 percent of U.S. sales; and we allowed 150 percent for international sales for 1972–1976. Applying the same technique as in the U.S. analysis, we again obtained low rates of return for the worldwide market. Anticipated low rates of return have also been indicated by Schwartzman, who developed an anticipated

TABLE 3

DISCOUNTED RETURN ON INVESTMENT

Average Sales Period	U.S. Market Profit margin assumption			Worldwide Markets Profit margin assumption		
	12%	15%	25%	12%	15%	25%
1962–66	3.5	5.9	11.7	6.9	9.4	15.8
1967–71	Neg.	Neg.	4.0	2.6	4.9	10.5
1972–76	Neg.	Neg.	2.5	3.0	5.3	11.1

TABLE 4

SALES NECESSARY TO ACHIEVE 10 AND 20 PERCENT RETURNS

Time Period	Number of New Chemical Entities	Sales Per Entity (millions of dollars)			
		10% Return		20% Return	
		15% profit margin	25% profit margin	15% profit margin	25% profit margin
1962–66	78	10.5	6.1	22.6	13.2
1967–71	63	19.1	11.2	42.0	24.5
1972–76	67	30.7	17.9	67.5	39.4

return of only 3 percent in 1973.[5] Clearly, on a worldwide basis, such low rates of return are not adequate to justify the risk inherent in pharmaceutical R&D.

By reversing our model, we have also calculated the required sales level necessary to achieve 10 and 20 percent returns on investment over a fifteen-year product life, assuming 15 and 25 percent profit margins. Table 4 shows how much required average sales levels have risen over time.

An analysis of the 194 new chemical entities introduced in the U.S. market during this fifteen-year period is summarized in Table 5. Nearly 71 percent of the products had average yearly worldwide sales of less than $10 million and only 6 percent had average sales levels in excess of $50 million. This demonstrates how difficult it would be to achieve the high sales levels the model calls for and how dependent the industry is on a relatively few large products.

On the basis of all available economic evidence and the implications from our research, we believe that the climate for research must improve considerably to encourage future innovation in the pharmaceutical industry. Economic incentives, including stronger patent protection and more favorable tax treatment for research, will be particularly important because of the increasingly difficult and complex scientific effort necessary to produce the next generations of pharmaceutical products.

Unfortunately, as Clarkson, Ladd, and MacLeod explain, the proposed Food and Drug Regulatory Reform Act would discourage

---

[5] David Schwartzman, *Pharmaceutical R&D Expenditures and Rates of Return* (Washington: American Enterprise Institute, 1974), p. 70.

TABLE 5

AVERAGE YEARLY WORLDWIDE SALES OF 194 NEW CHEMICAL ENTITIES

Worldwide Market (millions of dollars)	Number of Products	Percent of Total Products	Sales (millions of dollars)	Percent of Total Sales
0–10	137	70.6	424.0	14.3
10–20	16	8.3	213.4	7.2
20–30	14	7.2	374.0	12.7
30–40	8	4.1	316.0	10.7
40–50	7	3.6	330.0	11.2
50–60	4	2.1	240.0	8.1
70–80	4	2.1	310.0	10.5
80–90	1	0.5	84.0	2.9
100–200	2	1.0	360.0	12.2
200–300	1	0.5	300.0	10.2
Total	194	100.0	2,951.4	100.0

SOURCE: Author's estimates based on sales figures from IMS America.

pharmaceutical innovation in the U.S. market because companies could lose exclusivity in important international markets through early release of all safety and efficacy data. These authors further maintain that if such regulations were implemented in a smaller market, the industry might be forced to abandon or postpone entry into the local market rather than risk substantial losses in other countries.

As Parker indicates in his paper (Part III of this volume), pharmaceutical innovation has tended to concentrate in five countries: United States, United Kingdom, Switzerland, Japan, and West Germany. It seems no coincidence that these same countries have always encouraged a healthy climate for innovation and have had or are moving toward strong patent positions as an inducement for further innovation.

The pharmaceutical industry also has a significant disincentive toward innovation not shared by many other industries. Even after a patent position has been obtained, a waiting period of several years may ensue before the product is approved by the regulatory authorities. As the regulatory clearance time increases, the economic value of the patent right diminishes. Hence, it seems that a logical inducement for additional innovation would be to extend the patent life for pharmaceutical products, or to begin the patent life after approval is granted by the regulatory authorities for marketing the drug. In the United States, if the proposed Food and Drug Regulatory Reform legislation were to become law in its present form, and the drug clearance period be extended even further, an even more powerful case could be made for extension of the patent life or having the patent period begin upon FDA clearance. In economic terms, it seems clear that as increased regulatory hurdles appear, a quid pro quo must be created or the inducement for pharmaceutical innovation will diminish.

There are many signs that the U.S. technological position has been deteriorating with respect to its overseas competitors. For example, U.S. inventors were granted 45,633 patents by major trading partners in 1966, while the United States gave only 9,567 to foreign inventors. By 1976, the number of U.S. inventors granted patents abroad had dropped to 33,181, a 25 percent decline. The number of U.S. patents granted to foreigners in 1976 had almost doubled, to 18,744. In the pharmaceutical industry, a significant factor to be monitored closely is what appears to be a deterioration of the world market share held by U.S. firms.

It is clear that the United States will need robust high-technology industries capable of a strong export position in order to earn the foreign exchange necessary to pay for increasingly expensive commodity imports. Countries like Japan and West Germany have long recognized this problem and have conducted national economic programs accordingly. It seems clear that the United States now badly needs a coordinated national economic policy for high-technology industries, with the Food and Drug Administration, the National Science Foundation, Department of Commerce, Department of the Treasury, and industry working together rather than as adversaries. It is encouraging that government seems to be taking steps in this direction. The Carter administration has appointed a Domestic Policy Review Task Force, which will examine the impact on innovation of regulatory, tax, trade, antitrust, and procurement policy.

In conclusion, in view of rapidly rising research costs, increasing government regulations, and what we perceive to be a declining return on investment for the pharmaceutical industry, we believe that a more constructive worldwide attitude toward innovation is badly needed. In the United States, an improved climate is essential to encourage companies to undertake the high risks of innovative research.

Part Three

Medicines for the Third World

Pharmaceuticals and Third World Concerns: The Lall Report and the Otago Study

John E. S. Parker

At the University of Otago we have set ourselves the task of responding to the October 1975 report of the United Nations Conference on Trade and Development, *Major Issues in Transfer of Technology to Developing Nations: A Case Study of the Pharmaceutical Industry*— generally known as the Lall Report, after its author, Sanjaya Lall, of the Institute of Economics and Statistics at Oxford. Such a report would, almost of necessity, be inclined to reflect the viewpoint of the less developed nations. That is acceptable, but what is depressing, and the problem that has led to our response, is that Dr. Lall does not understand the economics of innovation. If the economics of innovation are not understood, all sorts of inappropriate conclusions may be reached— and are. I will detail some of these in this paper, as an introduction to our work at Otago.

I should make it clear first that I, unlike Schumpeter, do not separate innovation from invention: invention—both for the purposes of this paper and for those of our research effort—is merely a part (albeit the initial part) of innovation. Inventive activity (the "flash of genius" or the "act of insight") is subsumed under, and inextricably linked with, the entire innovative process.[1] My definitions do not substantially differ from Dr. Lall's, though of course he deplores many of the things I believe he should welcome.

Competitive Criteria

First of all, Dr. Lall assumes that the pharmaceutical industry should be measured by the usual "competitive" yardstick—that is, "competition" (which is his desideratum) is suggested by the absence: of high profits, of high submarket concentrations, and of patents as entry barriers. Specifically, he argues that the drug industry is marked by an

---

[1] See F. M. Scherer, *Industrial Market Structure and Economic Performance* (Chicago: Rand McNally, 1971), p. 350, and J. E. S. Parker, *The Economics of Innovation* (London: Longman, 1974), p. 19.

unusual degree of market power, even in comparison with other sectors that are increasingly dominated by multinational corporations, and that the implications of this power are more serious in the case of the pharmaceutical industry, because of the unique position that it occupies in saving human lives.[2] Note that his dedication to the principles of competition is based not on efficiency but on equity.

He goes on to measure the degree of competition by such traditional standards as concentration of production, price discrimination, high profits, and the heavy use of marketing tactics—all of these, in his view, show the absence of competition. But in the pharmaceutical industry, competition principally takes the form of rivalry in innovation—something that Dr. Lall overlooks (and that might, indeed, be *positively* related to heavy marketing expenditures, given certain assumptions about the process of innovation). The report spends considerable time demonstrating that there are high sales concentration ratios in particular pharmaceutical submarkets, as though the mere existence of these were sufficient to establish that the industry is monopolistic. It is not sufficient, and the time is not well spent.[3]

In fact, it is possible, and it may even be usual, to have high sales concentration accompanying high levels of economic rivalry. I use the expression "economic rivalry" with some care, to emphasize that in the pharmaceutical industry rivalry often takes the form of creating *and then eroding* monopoly through innovation. When this process is going on, entrenched monopoly is by definition unlikely, inasmuch as other firms will encroach upon the markets of the putative monopolist with superior—that is, innovative—products, rendering any great degree of market control temporary. Thus arises the anomaly: high concentration suggests monopoly but in fact reflects the dynamics of a particular process of competition.

What happens is that competition creates islands of monopoly and then subsequently destroys them. The appearance of these "monopolies" can be deceptive to the outside observer, and Dr. Lall would appear to have been so deceived. He is aware that the industry is innovative, but he argues that innovation destroys competition. Innovation, to him, is a means of creating or restoring monopoly, rather than part of a wider mechanism involving technological rivalry and the ebb and flow of market control by particular corporations.[4] When innovation is regarded

---

[2] United Nations Conference on Trade and Development, *Major Issues in Transfer of Technology to Developing Countries: A Case Study of the Pharmaceutical Industry* (hereinafter, *Lall Report*), TD/B/C.6/4 (Geneva: UNCTAD, 1975).

[3] Ibid., pp. 14–16, for the evidence on submarket concentration.

[4] Ibid., pp. 22–23, 59 (on patent protection).

as a weapon of monopoly, and high sales concentration regarded as a reflection of market power, it is hardly surprising that the pharmaceutical industry is considered suspect. But the suspicion is inappropriate.

It must be remembered that Lall is not attacking the presumed monopoly (or oligopoly) on the grounds that it is inefficient, but on the grounds that it is inequitable. He concludes that pharmaceutical industry concentration by country and concentration by company "not only raise the direct financial costs and indirect social costs, but also create important structural constraints upon the establishment of pharmaceutical industries, in the developing countries, primarily through the control of the required technology. . . ."[5] In his view, the direct costs include "the excessive profits earned by the transnational drug companies that result in the transfer of scarce foreign exchange resources" from the developing countries to the multinationals' home countries, as well as the R&D and marketing costs, which he says "contribute little to the real health needs of the vast majority of the developing world."[6] The indirect costs, in his view, include the "stifling of local pharmaceutical research and development . . . that would correspond better to real local health needs."[7] This last ties in with his views on marginal cost pricing, on which more later.

A Model of Innovation

To highlight Dr. Lall's treatment of the economics of innovation, let us consider the nature of his references to differentiation in the pharmaceutical industry. The large numbers of pharmaceuticals that come within given therapeutic subclasses occasion substantial adverse comment.[8] But this commentary, like his choice of competitive criteria, follows from his failure to appreciate the way in which innovation occurs. The flavor of Dr. Lall's remarks suggests that he expects innovation to be heroic, so that there will be only a few, though major, products developed in each therapeutic category. This expectation does not fit in with the generally accepted view of the way the process of innovation works in this and other industries (remembering, here, that I am defining innovation to include invention).[9] Typically, innovation comes about through the accumulation of a large number of minor changes—a process that,

---

[5] Ibid., p. vi.

[6] Ibid.

[7] Ibid.

[8] Ibid., pp. 30, 37, for example.

[9] J. Langrish, M. Gibbons, W. G. Evans, and F. R. Jevons, *Wealth From Knowledge* (London: Macmillan, 1972).

in the literature on the economics of innovation, is referred to as cumulative synthesis.[10] The "big step forward"—the transcendental event of heroic proportions—is rare. The usual process involves minor improvement on existing products and processes, with the emphasis on achieving small changes.

The point is worth attention. I have said elsewhere that "technology feeds on technology and in the process provides a major source of inventions" (or, in this case, of new drugs).[11] Techniques of application— new ways to use technology, or ways to use new technology—themselves amount to innovations. These techniques are not bequeathed to industry from outside but are part of the technological "know-how" developed within, and generally restricted to, the industry. Thus, it is entirely reasonable—indeed, it is to be expected—that innovation will be a step-by-step process.

Dr. Lall additionally misjudges the situation by implying that a process by which one company merely differentiates its drug from that of a competitor (or even from another of its own drugs) will necessarily produce a slow rate of technological change. Not only does this view show confusion between the size of the innovative step and the importance of the result, it also shows confusion between the size of the individual step and the overall rate of change, which, of course, includes a time variable. The rapid addition of many small—even trivial—advances can produce an impressive rate of technological change. Disparaging comments on pharmaceuticals as "me-toos" or on the process of developing new pharmaceuticals as "molecule manipulation" usually indicate profound misunderstanding of the way innovation comes about. The pharmaceutical industry is one in which product differentiation and cumulative synthesis are typical and in which technological progress has been rapid.

Though this situation holds true for many industries, in the pharmaceutical industry it may well be that government action reinforces the natural tendency to small-step advance. The regulation of innovation by public authorities, such as FDA in the United States and the Committee on Safety of Medicines in the United Kingdom, may be a significant brake on large-step new drug introductions. Where regulation is extremely cautious and involves long delays, company research managers may react by selecting new projects with the regu-

---

[10] A. P. Usher, *A History of Mechanical Inventions* (Cambridge, Mass.: Harvard University Press, 1954), and see also V. Ruttan, "Usher and Schumpeter on Invention, Innovation, and Technological Change," *Quarterly Journal of Economics*, vol. 73, no. 4 (November 1959), pp. 596–606.

[11] Parker, *Economics of Innovation*, p. 25.

lators in mind. That is, in order to make sure that new drug submissions are relatively quickly accepted, the manager may choose deliberately unambitious research projects. If innovation is thus confined to relatively minor departures from existing pharmacology, chances of long delay will be reduced, but the tendency toward small-step advance represented by cumulative synthesis processes will be strengthened. In this special sense that he does not intend, and in this sense only, Dr. Lall may well be correct in drawing our attention toward the industry's tendency toward "me-tooism." But the blame would then lie with the public authorities responsible for regulating pharmaceutical innovation, rather than with the multinational companies.

Marginal Cost Pricing

Perhaps Lall's most alarming argument is that pharmaceuticals should be available to Third World countries at marginal cost.[12] This argument implies that these nations neither will nor should contribute towards the cost of development for past or future pharmaceuticals, that they are only interested in those old drugs where development costs have already been fully recouped, and that this is all they ever will be interested in. It cannot be said that Dr. Lall alone holds these views. In recent years, there have been two major attempts to produce lists of essential drugs for the Third World—the Hathi report on the Indian pharmaceutical industry and the World Health Organization publication, *The Selection of Essential Drugs*.[13] Both lists are made up of basic pharmaceuticals that are old in commercial terms (for example, on the WHO list, not even ten are still under patent). But all this shows is that Dr. Lall is wrong in good company.

As far as I am aware, none of the drugs classed as essential was developed in the Third World—that is, the drugs that are essential to the less developed nations were produced by the advanced nations. Any expectation that new pharmaceuticals produced by the advanced nations are unlikely to be of interest to the developing countries would thus seem to fly in the face of experience. In fact, of course, these nations are providing, and presumably will continue to provide, a growing share of the world demand for drugs. It is not surprising then that the major companies are worried about the marginal cost argument: they could

---

[12] *Lall Report*, pp. 52–56.

[13] Ministry of Petroleum and Chemicals, *Report of the Committee on Drugs and Pharmaceutical Industry* (Delhi: Government of India, 1975), and World Health Organization, *The Selection of Essential Drugs*, WHO Technical Report no. 615 (Geneva: WHO, 1977).

not be expected to relish a situation in which a significant *and growing* portion of their market will not contribute to the costs of innovation.

In advocating marginal cost pricing, Dr. Lall may unwittingly be supporting a policy that will lower the future level of investment in new pharmaceuticals, and especially in those new pharmaceuticals that would be of interest chiefly to the Third World. He should be extremely cautious in appraising the trade-off between having present drugs available more cheaply (if, indeed, his recommendations would have that result) and having new drugs available in the future. It is not only the multinationals that should be leery of the marginal cost pricing argument.

Multinational Companies

Dr. Lall mistrusts the multinational company, and his concern is centered particularly on two areas: the concentration of research in a few developed home countries, and the ability of large corporations to engage in transfer pricing—that is, to charge high prices for intermediate goods in intracompany transfers, making high profits there, so as to show low profits (or to "require" high prices) in countries where profits are highly taxed (or in any less developed country). Pharmaceutical research is indeed concentrated in five main centers—the United States, the United Kingdom, Switzerland, West Germany, and Japan, which are also, of course, the home countries for most multinationals of whatever kind. Because research is thus concentrated, it is feared (not only by Dr. Lall) that in the future most new pharmaceutical developments will be of only peripheral relevance to the Third World. This ties in, of course, with Dr. Lall's view that competition does not exist in the drug industry, and his implicit view that, even if it did, it would be welcomed for its equity, not its efficiency. Moreover, it is quite true that in the absence of competition transfer pricing could be used to milk the less developed countries. The crucial question thus remains, Is there competition among multinational drug companies?

The Otago Research Project

In response to the Lall report, we at Otago University have decided to center our efforts in two areas: international price comparisons, and studies of the diffusion of new pharmaceuticals. We will be attempting to investigate the validity of the Third World fear of price exploitation (by the price comparisons) and the effect of the concentration of drug research and development and thus drug innovation (by the diffusion studies).

Third World Pharmaceutical Prices. In response to the concern among less developed countries that multinational enterprises have unwarranted power to impose arbitrary prices, we are carrying out a series of international price comparisons. These comparisons are intended to provide a factual basis for answering the question, Do Third World nations pay more for their drugs than the developed countries do? This study, at present, includes all those products common to New Zealand and each of six overseas markets. The prices used are those for January 1977, and the products currently included are those classified as "ethical" within New Zealand. Products that are sold in dissimilar strengths or that have minor dissimilarities whose therapeutic effect may be important are excluded. Prices are calculated per unit (as, for example, per ampule, capsule, tablet, gram (for cream), or milliliter (liquid), whichever is appropriate) at pharmacists' buying prices free of tax. Exchange rates are the average for the calendar year 1976.

What I am giving here is a preliminary report, which must be treated with extreme caution. Later on in the study, we will employ different comparisons—different techniques—and we will examine the impact of exchange rate movements (which in some cases, as for example Brazil, have been extreme). Tables 1 to 4 show the countries involved in our present comparisons, the numbers of drugs, the exchange rates used, and the composition of the sales by therapeutic class. The countries chosen are not entirely the same as those chosen by Dr. Lall to provide evidence of multinational control, though there is some overlapping. He notes, for example, that in Brazil in 1969 sixty-five

TABLE 1

NUMBERS OF PRODUCTS INCLUDED IN THE STUDY AND
PERCENTAGE PRICED HIGHER IN NEW ZEALAND, JANUARY 1977

Country	Products in Common with New Zealand	Percentage Higher priced in New Zealand
Venezuela	208	37
Indonesia	210	19
Australia	552	32
Philippines	197	23
United Kingdom	499	60
Brazil	225	45

SOURCE: M. H. Cooper, "World Pharmaceutical Prices 1977," provisional results (1) Otago University, 1978.

TABLE 2

OVERSEAS DRUG PRICES AS PERCENTAGE OF NEW ZEALAND PRICES

Country	All Drugs	Top Twenty (New Zealand)	Top Twenty (Overseas)
New Zealand	100	100	100
Venezuela	110	120	186
Australia	122	98	101
Philippines	138	96	—
United Kingdom	96	120	—
Brazil	83	88	77
Indonesia	—	128	83

SOURCE: Cooper, "World Pharmaceutical Prices 1977."

TABLE 3

EXCHANGE RATES AGAINST THE U.S. DOLLAR, 1970 AND 1976

Country	1970	1976	Percent Change
Australia (dollars)	0.8976	0.8178	−8.9
Brazil (cruzeiros)	4.594	10.673	132.3
Indonesia (rupiah)	378.50	416.00	9.9
New Zealand (dollars)	0.8899	0.8998	1.1
Philippines (pesos)	5.907	7.496	26.9
United Kingdom (pounds)	0.41736	0.5540	32.8
Venezuela (bolivares)[a]	n.a.	4.932	—

[a] Venezuela July 1976 4.932 Bs per $(US) to June 1977 5.0045 Bs per $(US). Percent change for period = 1.5.

multinational drug companies held 88 percent of the market (Brazil, by the way, does not allow drugs to be patented) and that in the Philippines in 1966 multinationals held more than 80 percent of the market (both being figures generally representative of the third world). But he does not provide data for Indonesia or Venezuela (unless the latter is included among the "Central American countries" where the multinational market share is more than 80 percent).[14] New

---

[14] *Lall Report*, pp. 18–19.

TABLE 4

Sales of Pharmaceuticals by Therapeutic Class as Percentage of Total Ethical Sales (December 1976 or January 1977)

Class	New Zealand	Australia	Brazil	Indonesia	Philippines	Venezuela
Alimentary Tract and Metabolism	10.4	14.2	24.9	21.2	18.6	23.4
Blood and Blood Forming Organs	0.8	1.4	3.2	3.4	3.3	4.2
Cardiovascular System	21.1	18.9	7.6	3.5	2.8	6.4
Dermatologicals	7.6	5.9	6.1	5.6	7.3	10.2
Genito-Urinary System and Sex Hormones	5.6	6.9	7.5	2.3	1.1	6.6
Systemic Hormonal Preparations (excl. sex hormones)	0.7	1.0	2.0	4.3	4.0	2.8
General anti-Infectives Systemic	16.1	16.7	15.9	29.7	25.1	15.8
Musculo-Skeletal System	5.8	6.7	4.1	4.3	2.5	3.7
Central Nervous System	16.5	13.6	10.1	9.9	8.3	8.7
Parasitology	1.0	0.8	2.0	0.9	0.9	1.5
Respiratory System	12.5	11.4	11.1	11.6	15.8	10.5
Sensory Organs	1.5	2.1	1.9	1.5	0.4	1.7
Various	0.5	0.6	3.7	1.6	10.1	4.5

Source: M. H. Cooper, "World Pharmaceutical Prices 1977."

Zealand, Australia, and the United Kingdom are of course being used here for comparative purposes.

As time passes, we will be carrying out full price comparisons on the entire WHO list of essential drugs—comparisons per unit package, comparisons weighted by sales value in home and overseas markets, comparisons by therapeutic group, comparisons adjusted for exchange rate movements (not merely for average exchange rates). We will also be looking at prices not only in monetary terms but in terms of the hours of work needed to earn the price of the drug. We will be looking at national per capita expenditure on pharmaceuticals. We also will be adding other countries to our list, and we will not be restricting ourselves to 1976–1977. And in the end, of course, when we have finished the study, we will consider the problems inherent in making such international comparisons.

Obviously, all comment must be tentative until the work in progress is completed, and results to date do not permit any firm conclusions. Our study thus far provides neither confirmation nor denial of the fear of the developing nations that they pay more than their advanced counterparts for the drugs they buy. Preliminary results neither support nor deny what is, we must remember, a very natural worry.

Diffusion Studies. It is plausible to assert that the presence of multinational companies in the industry will speed up the worldwide spread of pharmaceutical innovations. Foreign subsidiaries of these multinationals will have technological endowments independent of those of their host nations and will also have the commercial insurance provided by their parent-company backing. Their awareness of new products and technologies and their ability to introduce them are likely to be similar to, if not the same as, those of the parent companies. In a Third World country, the difference between a subsidiary of a foreign multinational and its native host-country counterpart is likely to be enormous, and this difference alone might well make the alien a potent agent of diffusion. When the superior "appropriation" qualities of foreign direct investment (as compared with exporting or licensing) are added to the list of advantages, it becomes virtually certain that diffusion will be expedited by the existence of the multinational pharmaceutical firms. Pharmaceutical innovation may tend to be concentrated in five main centers, but manufacture and distribution tend to be based on a worldwide network of foreign affiliates. Given the presence of the multinational form of organization, the intercountry spread of innovation not only should be rapid, but it should occur at a rate dictated by the health needs—not the technological awareness—of the recipient economy.

In general, we expect that the lag in drug introduction in recipient economies should be a function of the size of the market in the recipient economies, the size of the innovative step involved, the profitability of the market in the recipient economies, the form of the diffusing agent (whether a subsidiary of a multinational, a sales agent, or an independent company), the regulatory tightness of the recipient economies, and the technological background there.[15] In an attempt to throw light on the factors that influence the intercountry rate of diffusion of pharmaceutical innovations, we are collecting data on introduction times—the time a product is first sold commercially in a given country. We hope to be able to identify these dates for as many countries and as many drugs as possible. We expect that certain cases will prove particularly interesting. In Japan, for example, internal foreign direct investment has been rare, so the diffusion has been carried out almost entirely by licensing and emulation; we hope to find significant contrasts between introduction times in Japan and those elsewhere.

The selection of drugs for inclusion in the sample is based on the WHO report, *The Selection of Essential Drugs*. This report lists, by generic name, those pharmaceuticals deemed by the advisory panel to be essential to the primary health care requirements of developing nations. We are confining our sample to drugs from this list for three reasons. First, the list (despite my strictures on it in the first part of this paper) does represent an attempt to identify a common core of basic needs, universally relevant and applicable to developing nations. Second, the developing nations will judge the performance of the world's pharmaceutical companies according to their ability to deliver drugs that meet their needs. Third, the use of this list will avoid the charge that our diffusion studies include drugs that are peripheral to the requirements of developing nations.

Unfortunately, the translation of generic names to brand names in order to identify product introduction dates is an enormously time-consuming and labor-intensive task. The project was begun in May 1978 and at the time of this conference (September 1978) is still incomplete. We have now collected introduction dates on a limited number of products from the WHO list, though not enough to be able to determine (1) the average lag (by therapeutic class) between the

---

[15] That is, we will be testing the equation $D = f(S, I, P, A, R, T)$, where D is the lag, S the size of the market, I the size of the innovative step, P the profitability, A the form of the agent (dummy variable), R the regulatory tightness, and T the technological background.

original introduction and the subsequent spread to recipient economies, (2) the geographical route taken in the process of diffusion, or (3) the intercountry diffusion rates, using Japan as the "nonmultinational" standard of measurement.

We anticipate, though, that the diffusion lag between the main centers of innovation and the developing countries may be short. Differences between introduction dates for a given pharmaceutical may well be measured in months rather than years, especially where the transfer is effected within a multinational corporation. It is expected that diffusion times will be longer where multinationals are not involved.

Concluding Remarks

The developing countries, as the Lall report makes quite clear, feel vulnerable to the pharmaceutical multinationals—more so than to multinationals in other lines. They fear price exploitation and suspect that the way drug innovation is concentrated within the developed countries implies that the research needed on the particular health requirements of the Third World will be neglected. The international pricing study as carried out thus far suggests that the exploitation hypothesis is neither proved nor disproved. The diffusion studies may reveal some evidence relevant to the "health needs/centralized research" argument, but it is too early to say. If it is established that the multinational corporation is a potent diffusion agent, then this should at least temper Third World mistrust. A demonstration that pharmaceuticals defined as essential by the WHO list reach the developing nations quickly may add a new perspective to the debate.

Commentary

Stephen P. Magee

High technology represents a high risk operation. The multinational corporations justifiably feel that the developing countries, as Professor Parker has said, really do not understand the process of technology creation. A 1,000 percent return on a successful innovation can be perfectly consistent with competitive rates of return. With a 1-in-100 success ratio, that would work out to about a 10 percent expected rate of return. But the LDCs forcus on the anomalies—the 1,000 percent returns—without understanding the total process. The point of having trade secrets and patents is to create monopolists, and we should not be surprised when someone exercises the seventeen-year monopoly right they have been given. The less developed countries are frustrated with the second-best monopoly policy: in the world of worlds we might want, there would be no need to have private markets given over to monopolists for a time in order to generate innovation.

In a second-best world the alternative to monopoly would be public involvement in the provision of pharmaceuticals. There are deadweight losses in having goods distributed by monopolists because we know that monopolists undersupply goods relative to the social optimum. Government R&D with free dissemination of the idea generates an optimal output once a new good is developed, but the problem is that governments, by and large, do not know what goods people need and want. Government bureaucracies have a hard time determining how to allocate R&D funds. Private markets, in contrast, have a better idea where to put research money, but once they have produced a new good, they undersupply it for some period of time.

We should also look at the problems on the private side. Private-market creation of pharmaceuticals (as of other new products) does generate a problem. What is privately profitable may not be socially optimal—something Professor Parker is well aware of, as is shown in

147

his work related to appropriability problems in *The Economics of Innovation*.[1] We get into a number of other interesting problems here for the developed countries vis-à-vis the developing countries in the production of high-technology goods.

For example, in general, private-market creation of such quasi-public goods as new information or new technology produces more sophisticated results than would be produced by public-sector creation —simply because private profitability is higher for complicated items than for noncomplicated items. Therefore, a firm creating a new process or a new product has to worry about having it taken away and thus will make it more sophisticated to improve its appropriability. This point holds in varying degrees for different pharmaceuticals. Trade secrets will provide high appropriability for "sophisticated pharmaceuticals" whose composition cannot be determined by chemical analysis. R&D will be higher in these areas, ceteris paribus.

There is also a lot of misunderstanding about monopoly. Briefly, as I understand it, the mechanism works something like this: monopolistic and oligopolistic industries raise barriers to entry that encourage innovation because they allow supernormal prices for some period of time and therefore generate monopoly profits. Now, those monopoly profits, as Professor Parker noted, are competed away by multinationals (or any firms) not by price competition per se but by research and development. The development of new drugs erodes— competes away—the monopoly profits; that is, we have competition by innovation.

This is not, of course, the only view of the way the process works. In my work on pricing technologies, I have come across some anomalies.[2] For example, a multinational creating a new technology must worry how fast it can be stolen, or how fast it can be copied either legally or nonlegally. The faster the monopoly erodes, the lower the profit in creating that technology, all other things being equal. And if the multinational, in pharmaceuticals or anything else, adopts a high-price strategy—say IBM develops a new computer and charges a very high price for it—the high price induces copying and increases the speed with which the technology will be emulated by rivals.

The trade-off is thus between a high-price strategy with large profits today and less tomorrow, versus a low-price one with low profits

[1] John E. S. Parker, *The Economics of Innovation* (London: Longman, 1974).

[2] Stephen P. Magee, "Application of the Dynamic Limit Pricing Model to the Price of Technology and International Technology Transfer," in K. Brunner and A. Meltzer, eds., *Optimal Policies, Control Theory and Technology Exports* (New York: North-Holland, 1977), pp. 203–244.

today and more tomorrow, the latter emerging from less emulation. As it so often is, the trade-off is between present profits and future profits. The pricing strategy that maximizes the total present discounted value of the new innovation is simply a downward sloping price trajectory through time. Another property is that the optimum price in the short run is always less than the short-run monopoly price. This problem has already been presented and solved in the industrial organization literature by Darius Gaskins[3] and I have modified and applied his model to technology problems.

An interesting result emerges from the comparative statics of the technology-creation process for any one of four government policies directed toward multinationals that reduce the current price for existing technology. The policies would transfer more technology to the developing countries because the price goes down so LDCs can buy more of the technology; but when innovating firms lower today's price (and thereby transfer more technology), their long-run market share increases.

Consider two of these policies. Suppose we lengthen patent lives (instead of shortening patent lives as the developing countries want). The multinational would then look at future profits relative to present profits and conclude "Tomorrow's profits are now worth more to us, so to protect them, we will lower today's price." The more one is concerned about the future, the more one wants to keep copiers out. And one strategy of keeping them out is to shift to a lower price trajectory. Consider another: if we were to revise the Paris Convention, as the developing countries would like, and increase the speed of entry for emulators, we would paradoxically increase the market share of a large firm like IBM. The faster we let people copy technology, the more the overall amount of innovation taking place will be reduced, because innovation will have become less profitable. And the reduction in innovation will be concentrated in the large firm.

But it turns out, when IBM cuts the price of a new computer optimally as a result of increased competition, the decrease in price more than offsets the increased rapidity of emulation. In the long run, the more rapidly IBM's computer technology is copied, the more IBM will cut the price and increase its long-run market share. Thus, in some cases, policies advocated by the LDCs will make multinationals more dominant, because of the mathematics of optimal pricing.

---

[3] Darius Gaskins, "Dynamic Limit Pricing: Optimal Pricing Under Threat of Entry," *Journal of Economic Theory*, vol. 3 (1971), pp. 306–322.

Let me finish by reporting one other result from some of my own unpublished work. I have been concerned, as Professor Parker has, as to whether firm size provides an important "appropriability" mechanism.[4] One cannot simply say that large firms innovate more, or even that they innovate less: the results are industry specific. We have to look at industry structure. And when we look at the appropriability mechanism within industries, and at the way innovation is correlated with firm size—and when we tie that in with the comparative advantage of the developing country—we discover that firm size is more closely tied to innovation for industries in which the developing countries have a comparative advantage than for other industries. It is in the standardized goods industries that innovation varies with firm size, sometimes positively and sometimes negatively. In some standardized goods industries it is the small firm that carries out the innovation, while in others the larger firms dominate. Contrariwise, with new and sophisticated products (such as pharmaceuticals), there is no significant relationship between firm size and innovation; other appropriability mechanisms exist.

This is an area where there is a great deal of work to be done. What Professor Parker is trying to determine, I take it, is this: If there is a monopolized or quasimonopolized industry in which new technology is being created, with monopoly profits used as the carrot to induce innovation, and if the sellers of the new high technology are perfectly discriminating monopolists, then can the monopolist—in this case, the multinational—extract the entire area under the demand curve for the life of the patent? This is a question apart from determining the optimal pricing model. Take a simple static case in which the monopolist can extract the whole area under the demand curve. There is no surplus to the buyer: he pays ten dollars for what generates ten dollars in value for him. It seems to me that this is really the issue between the multinationals and the developing countries. The developing countries—the buyers—believe that they get none of the surplus and they feel that it is important that some of the surplus be shared with them.

The price discrimination question is difficult conceptually and it is difficult to know how much of the surplus is shared by the developing countries. Professor Parker's data throw some light on this situation in the pharmaceutical industry.

---

[4] "Appropriability" refers to the extent to which the social return on an innovation is reflected in private returns: the lower the private return relative to the social return, the lower the appropriability.

John Jennings

I would be out of my depth if I were to attempt to discuss the economic incentives for innovation or distribution, so I will go back to the title of the discussion, "Medicines for Third World Markets." The concerns I hear voiced over and over again by the representatives of the less developed countries are roughly these:

First, about the cost of drugs: the point is made that in these countries, pharmaceuticals constitute as much as 40 percent of health care costs, as against about 7 percent in the developed countries. Indeed, even among the least developed of the Americas, the cost of drugs in the health care system rarely exceeds 10 or 12 percent.

Second, about the appropriateness for particular needs and the safety and efficacy of the drugs: the question is raised of the applicability of drugs to the health conditions that exist in the less developed countries, along with some issues that might seem peripheral, such as the promotional practices firms use to penetrate the market.

Finally, about the quality of drugs provided to the less developed countries, as expressed in the so-called dumping syndrome: one gets the impression almost of paranoia and a search for simple solutions to complex problems—a national industry, excessive reliance on regional control laboratories, even a turning to medicinal plants as an alternate resource in health care.

It occurs to me that these are only somewhat exaggerated expressions of what we hear in this country. We too hear complaints about the cost of drugs and about premiums going to those who have taken the lead in research and innovation. But there are some real differences between what is perceived by the developed countries, by the industry, and by the governments of the less developed countries.

There is one chart I would like to see, regarding price comparisons between developed and less developed countries, and that is the percentage of health care costs represented by drugs—whether prices measured this way, for example, are essentially the same in Indonesia and the Philippines, two countries that are not especially "less developed." Drug costs may represent an inordinate proportion of overall health care costs, even if the actual cost of the drugs is not much (or any) higher than in the developed countries.

Moreover, in the less developed countries, in many instances, there is a marked difference between relatively affluent urban dwellers and people in the countryside. Over and over again, in the capital cities of the less developed countries, where a relatively large percentage of the population may be concentrated, the people—especially the wealthy

151

people—do have access to health care and to sophisticated drugs. Frequently, they demand and receive drugs that are not essential—fad drugs, mood drugs, tonics and vitamins, and terrible mixtures of that sort—while out in the countryside there are people in need of simple antibiotics and other basic drugs. That pattern of distribution is quite different from what it is in more developed nations.

In addition, there is a tremendous attraction to high technology in the less developed countries, and this sometimes distorts the pattern of their investment in health care supplies and pharmaceuticals. For example, one will find people who are extremely competent and highly qualified in, say, renal dialysis in a country where they could provide maintenance for several thousand patients at the most. And this will be a dead-end situation because the country has not yet achieved the technology required for the next step (which, here, would be transplants). At the same time, at the other end of the spectrum, the few dollars that are needed for antibiotics to prevent streptococcal disease—which leads to the terminal renal failure—are not made available. Those who are in control are enamored of the gadgetry and high technology rather than penicillin, a common drug that has been around since 1941.

This important and all-too-human factor is not always addressed in considering the problem of the innovation, distribution, and the cost of drugs in less developed countries. Just as Dr. Lall has had a vision since he prepared his report, I hope that the governments of the less developed countries—and most of them do have some centralized regulation of medical practice and distribution of pharmaceuticals—will begin to appreciate that they cannot expect to achieve quickly the same level of sophisticated technology as the United States, Britain or Japan. They will have to make the best use of what is currently available, because some advanced innovation is beyond their means or not as important as other needs.

It seems to be taken for granted that the developed countries should assist the less developed countries in any number of ways. I think that medicines represent a legitimate area for sharing. How this sharing is to be done, I would not venture to suggest, except to say that without any interference from government, there should be an effort to provide the Third World countries with what they need at a cost that they can afford. Whether this precludes the research premium and whether it means, in effect, subsidizing the export of drugs, or pricing them at the marginal level are questions that people more skilled in economics than I will have to work out. But we should recognize that there is a problem, one that—along with such comparable problems as nutrition and water supply—we must address. It is clearly in our own interest to improve the health and general well-being of the less developed countries.

William Treharne

First of all, I would like to agree with Dr. Jennings that there is an urgent need to have essential pharmaceutical products available in the Third World. And I know the pharmaceutical industry has played and will continue to play a significant role in making these products available.

Of the two aspects of Dr. Parker's research—pricing and diffusion —I would like to dwell on the second. The World Health Organization, the United Nations Industrial Development Organization, the United Nations Conference on Trade and Development, and other United Nations authorities—through such people as Professor Lall—are particularly looking at ways to improve the diffusion of essential drugs in the Third World.

Professor Lall just published another booklet, this one through UNIDO, *The Growth of the Pharmaceutical Industry in Developing Countries: Problems and Prospects.*[1] In this paper, he indicates that the diffusion of pharmaceutical products can be achieved by establishing pharmaceutical production units in the developing countries. And he uses some fairly simple approaches in his study—approaches that should be commented on.

First of all, Lall uses a population of 3 million as the base on which one could establish a domestic pharmaceutical industry. It is true that a base of 3 million could include enough patients with enough diseases to provide the market for a pharmaceutical plant. The problem is that in many of the developing countries there is no infrastructure to get the products to the people in the outlying areas. I have had the opportunity of living and working in many of these countries, and I can testify from experience that there is a complete lack of this essential infrastructure. Clinics, hospitals, doctors, and nurses are almost nonexistent—not only in the crowded cities but also in the scattered hinterland. In a number of these countries there may be only one doctor for 300,000 people. It is impractical to use a base figure of 3 million, or any figure, until the illness can be properly diagnosed and the needed therapeutic product can be delivered to the patient.

Dr. Lall goes on to say that the industry could be established at

---

[1] United Nations Industrial Development Organization, *The Growth of the Pharmaceutical Industry in Developing Countries: Problems and Prospects*, U.N. publication no. E.78.II.B.4 (New York: United Nations, 1978).

first in a simple formulation and packaging plant. This probably is a practical first step in many of the developing countries. But UNIDO, and others, are looking at the matter from the wrong perspective, using as examples countries such as Burundi, the Cape Verde Islands, or the Central African Republic, which barely have (or do not have) populations of 3 million. This is not to belittle the attempts being made in this regard, only to highlight the difficulties.

Let me use as an example the difficulty we as a company have faced in establishing a simple formulation and packaging plant in Nigeria, which is more sophisticated than, say, the Central African Republic. The construction of the plant itself presented tremendous difficulties because of the lack of suitable land, water, roads, electricity, and so on. There was a lack of architects, engineers, construction workers, and subcontractors, and such things as cement or fittings for doors. I am not saying these problems cannot be overcome, but one should be aware of them.

Moreover, the production even of relatively simple drugs requires such things as bottles, vials, and packaging material. The equipment to be put into the new plant is relatively sophisticated, and the local supply of bottles or vials will probably not meet the specifications on such sophisticated imported machinery. In order to maintain continuous production, then, there will be a need for an ancillary industry within the country.

When the manufacture of the product is begun, the all-important aspect of quality control will come into play. Policies and procedures will be needed to ensure high-quality effective medicines—there cannot be any slippage in this respect—which means the country will need well-trained and educated people and elaborate scientific equipment to test the products. One must determine also whether there are people available locally to service this equipment, and generally the needed technicians are simply not available in these less developed countries. This, again, is just a warning of problems one can encounter.

Dr. Lall goes on to argue that the basic manufacture of essential pharmaceuticals, such as penicillins and tetracyclines, should be achievable in some of the larger developing countries, such as India, Brazil, Turkey, Egypt, and Mexico. There have been attempts in India, in Pakistan, in Egypt, and in a few other countries to carry out the basic manufacture of narrow-spectrum antibiotics like penicillins and the streptomycins, but I know from personal experience that they have run into problems in trying to produce a quality product. Even if this problem is overcome (which it often has been), then they find the cost of the product is invariably higher than the cost of products available from the developed countries. For example, the Indian streptomycin prices have been as high as ten times world market prices; they are now down to a lower figure but nowhere near as low as the world price.

Dr. Lall also suggests an exchange of information on technology between those countries that have established a basic manufacturing industry and those countries that have not. This to me represents an oversimplification. The multinational corporations (which produce such products as penicillins), maintain constant research and development programs to improve their output and reduce their costs. They are unlikely to exchange such valuable information. This continuing research and development unfortunately does not go on in some of the developing countries where these basic production units have been established. This is not to say that assistance would not be provided by multinational corporations. I know our company has offered assistance to the governments of Egypt and India and would be prepared to help elsewhere in getting the products to the people, but it would not be assistance that involves giving up trade secrets.

On the question of diffusion, Dr. Lall suggests centralized purchasing and refers to a particular case study by Professor Bibile on centralized purchasing in Sri Lanka.[2] We have a plant in Sri Lanka, and we know just how successful the Sri Lanka centralized purchasing system was. It brought about poor product quality, an oversupply of some products, and an undersupply of other products, and it did not save foreign exchange. This has been pointed out to Sri Lanka and the United Nations, without killing the hope that centralized purchasing could help a developing country.

Dr. Lall's UNIDO report suggests that the marketing and distribution of pharmaceutical products is fairly simple. But it is not simple in these developing countries. Take Ethiopia, for example, a country of about 30 million people spread throughout a countryside that is one of the most rugged one could possibly come across. Getting a constant supply of drugs into this countryside would be very difficult indeed. There are not many roads, there are few airports, and there is little in the way of rail transport. Even if hospitals, clinics, and nurses existed to diagnose these widely dispersed people, how would the diagnosis and the drugs be delivered where there is no internal delivery system? This is just an example of what one needs to consider before reaching the conclusion that a pharmaceutical plant is feasible.

---

[2] S. Bibile, *Case Studies in Transfer of Technology: Pharmaceutical Policies in Sri Lanka*, U.N. report no. TD/B/C.6/21, (Geneva: UNCTAD, 1977).

155

Reference was made to the availability of local herbs and plants for possible use in medicines and treatment of the ill—pyrethrum, say, to kill mosquitos, and cinchona for quinine. This makes some sense, but it overlooks the fact that pyrethrum is only grown in certain altitudes in certain climatic conditions. Indeed, only two or three countries in the world—one being Kenya, and another being Tanzania—produce most of the supply of pyrethrum, while cinchona is only grown, that I know of, in Indonesia and Sri Lanka and one country in Latin America.

I do not mean to be overly critical, but I want to emphasize that there are many difficulties in achieving the objective. We, as people coming from the industrialized world, the developed world, want to help the United Nations and the developing countries make drugs available as widely as possible, but there are difficulties in the suggested approaches. We appreciate the urgent need throughout the developing world for readily diffused, inexpensive, effective, and easy-to-administer pharmaceutical products. But the construction of a modern pharmaceutical plant to produce these products is only one of the essential steps. Not only must it be possible to manage and maintain this unit efficiently with qualified and experienced people and efficient machinery, it must also be possible to deliver the product to the sick and ailing, wherever they may be, through a medical/clinical distribution infrastructure.

A Note on the Book

The typeface used for the text of this book is Times Roman, which was designed by Stanley Morison. The type was set by Maryland Linotype Composition Company, of Baltimore. Braun-Brumfield, Inc., of Ann Arbor, Michigan, printed and bound the book, using paper manufactured by the S.D. Warren Company. The cover and format were designed by Pat Taylor, and the figures were drawn by Hördur Karlsson.

The manuscript was edited by Janet Marantz and by Elizabeth Ashooh, of the AEI Publications staff.